# *High Sierra* FLY FISHING

*Basics to Advanced Tactics*          ·*Billy Van Loek*

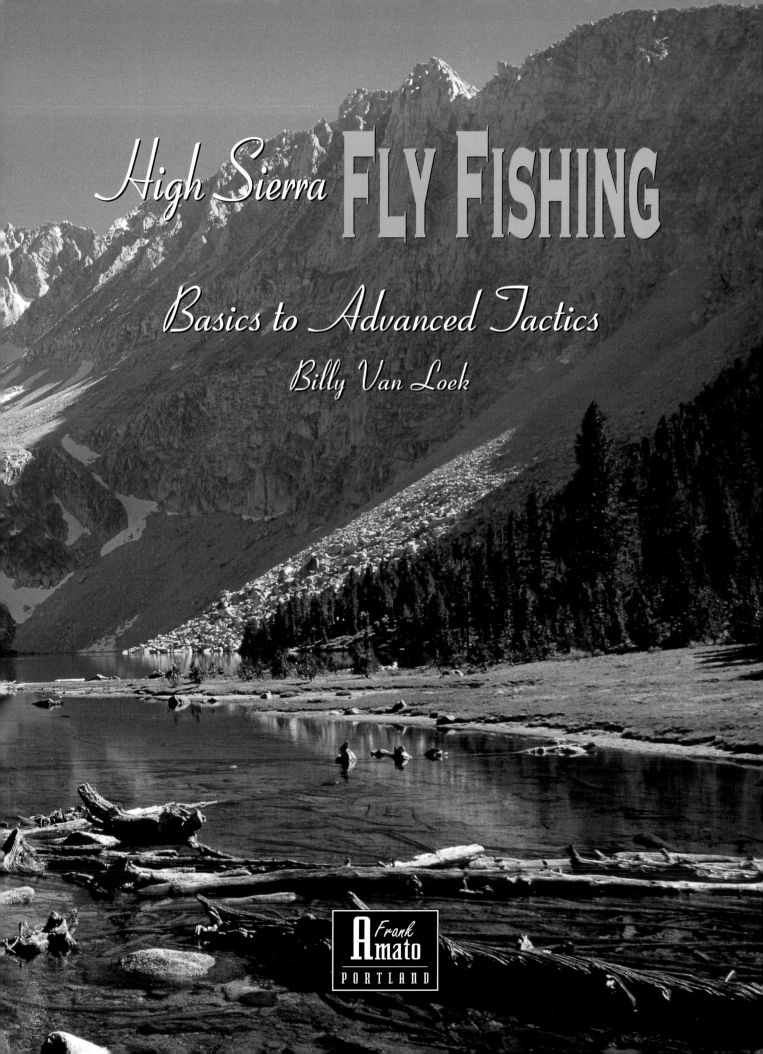

# High Sierra FLY FISHING

## Basics to Advanced Tactics

### Billy Van Loek

Frank Amato
PORTLAND

# In Memorium

Bob Jackson, a high school friend, gave his life in Vietnam for the cause of freedom.

# Acknowledgements

Thanks to: My nephew, Davy Miller, for giving me the idea for this book and urging me to write it; My nephews, Len and Paul Mayer and Patrick Phillips, who were my pupils in the school of the wild; My older sisters—Mary Mayer for her artwork and Susan Miller for proofreading not once but twice; My friend Edward Norton Ward for reminiscing with me about mountaineering and offering to tie a couple of the old patterns he once tied by the gross to put himself through college; Darrell Wong, CDFG, for speaking with me about trout; Winston Rod Co. and Ernie's Casting Pond, Soquel CA, for a trial of Winston's five-piece rod. Last but not least, thanks to Frank Amato for taking a chance on my first book.

The author is a naturalist by avocation and an attorney-litigator by trade. He is in the process of finishing the pup shown in the photo who had a 5-bird day on her first pheasant hunt.

Published in 2001 by Frank Amato Publications, Inc.
P.O. Box 82112, Portland, Oregon 97282
(503) 653-8108 • www.amatobooks.com

Softbound ISBN: 1-57188-217-0
Softbound UPC: 0-66066-00431-4
Hardbound ISBN: 1-57188-222-7
Hardbound UPC: 0-66066-00436-9

All photographs taken by the author unless otherwise noted.
Processing C&I Photography

Fly Illustrations: Mary Mayer
Figures 2, 3, 7 and knots: Brian Griffiths
Traditional Captain, California Coachman & Grey Hackle Yellow tied
by Edward Norton Ward; all other flies by author.
Layout: Tony Amato

Printed in Singapore

10  8  6  4  2    3  5  7  9

# Contents

# *Introduction*

*I* recall a day a few years ago fly-fishing along the shoreline of a High Sierra lake near treeline. The smooth lake reflected the surrounding peaks, tipped with the light of dawn. No one was about except a young man on the far shore. The morning was still except for the muted splash of his spinner, as he fished from a rock in front of a screen of wind-battered lodgepole pines. A column of wood smoke rising behind the trees gave away his party's campsite.

I worked my way around into the shadows that held one side of the lake and cast a dry fly to rising trout near the shore. I had forgotten the other angler as I caught and released seven or eight fish in about an hour. Light began to fill the cirque and the rises tapered off. I began walking the shore, searching the water hoping to see fish cruising. I spotted one crossing a flat over a smattering of water grass. I had earlier tied on a nymph, thinking I'd be casting to deeper water. I quickly cast ahead of him anyway, letting the heavy fly settle onto the bottom. When the trout approached, I twitched the fly, sending a tiny cloud of silt across his path. He immediately rushed the fly, I lifted the rod tip and had him on!

I let him play a little, and after his initial struggle he tried to tow the line away. I quickly stripped line and pulled him to my feet. He was a vividly colored wild brook trout about twelve inches. His white-edged, vermillion fins glowed as he flared them in the morning light, crimson dots in blue-gray haloes spattered his glistening yellow-olive sides as he turned on his side in the shallows. As I lifted him out of the water to back the hook out of the corner of his jaw his mottled dark-green dorsal fin folded flat over his vermiculated back. I was about to release him when I turned and realized the young man had walked around the lake.

The fish darted away, and we struck up a conversation. From his wistful confession I learned that, despite fishing every day, he had caught only one small fish on a salmon egg. "Real small," he said, after seeing the fish I released. "You sure are having great luck." I noted his gear. He was rigged with a #2 blade spinner with a treble hook and what appeared to be ten-pound line that would have been a fine set-up for black bass down in the foothills at New Melones or Pardee Reservoir. I could see discouragement in his eyes, when he asked how it could be so easy to catch so many trout.

The secret was that I had taught myself how to fly-fish the High Sierra after I started backpacking in college. I took along my old spinning gear at first and had the same realization as the young man, that my spinning gear was too much for any of the water except the really big lakes, and more often just scared the trout. By trial and error I figured out you had to use what is now known as ultra-light spinning tackle to catch many trout. I had heard of fly-fishing but I didn't know anyone who used a fly rod or even see many fly-fishers on the trail.

Although I decided fly-fishing was the way to go, I didn't have much money for equipment much less guides or lessons. Instead, I found a copy of Roderick Haig-Brown's *Primer of fly fishing* in the Berkeley City Library. That and a $7.00 fly rod from Sears got me started.

The *Primer* is now out of print and the technical information about rods and lines is out of date. But Roderick Haig-Brown, who lived in Canada, was one of the great men of fly-fishing, and every word it contains about fishing is valuable. He wrote several other books about fly-fishing that are highly regarded. His *Primer* was the inspiration for this one.

Another great man of fly-fishing, Edward R. Hewitt, said there are three stages in an angler's development:

When he wants to catch all the fish he can.

When he strives to catch the largest fish.

When he studies to catch the most difficult fish he can find, requiring the greatest skill and most refined tackle . . .

This book is for anyone ready for level one—catching a lot of trout on a hiking trip to the California High Sierra mountains. I consider the High Sierra to be the best possible place to learn to fly-fish, since you can focus on the fish with a minimum of distraction over fly selection, equipment, theory or intimidation from more skilled anglers, and it's easy to find uncrowded streams and lakes.

But this book isn't limited to basics or beginners. I will share my hard-won secrets of success fishing the High Sierra, so there are plenty of tips and advanced techniques tailored to the mountains. And I included some hints for finding bigger trout.

This book is not about the artistic qualities of fly-fishing. It is a practical book about fishing and how to think about trout. fly-fishing is not necessarily "greener," nor is it mystical, ennobling or most of the other hype written about it. In the context of the waters of the High Sierra, it is a more effective method of fishing. To be sure, wild trout are wonderfully marked and colored fish and a pleasure to fly-fish for in a wilderness setting. But what matters most is they are instinctive creatures with known patterns of behavior that can be learned. Knowing a little trout science brings success in the sport of fly-fishing.

I can't teach anyone fly-casting with this book. That has to be learned by doing. I discuss fly-casting, and describe the basic casts an angler needs to know to effectively fish the High Sierra. But you will need to find casting instruction before you head out on a trip to the High Sierra. If you don't, you can count on a lot of frustration and aggravation once you get there. I know, I did it the hard way.

I make recommendations for gear and include a chapter on backpacking. There is an appendix with information on obtaining maps and wilderness permits and a bibliography which includes Internet resources.

But the most important thing is the fishing. Using the concepts and techniques presented in this book, you will catch trout if you adventure into the California High Sierra. And not just a few trout. You will catch and release many wild trout in a granitic wonderland of coldwater lakes and streams, wind-sculpted pines and knife-edged crags, a land where you can wander under open skies and need only courage for a guide.

—*Billy Van Loek*
Carmel Valley, CA

# Chapter 1

# How The Trout Got There: Basic Fishing Biology And Geology of The High Sierra

*Nude ranges reared above glaciated valleys where not a green thing lived but a few thin patches of hair grass and some little red and yellow flowers. A built-up, rampart-like trail led into the steep chasm below.*

*—Charles McDermand*

## DEFINING THE HIGH SIERRA

The following definition is given for the High Sierra by Professors Storer and Usinger in *Sierra Nevada Natural History*:

"The term High Sierra applies properly to the alpine region above the main forest (about 8000+ ft.), where peaks, lake basins, and other rock structures carved by glaciation are conspicuous. It extends about 150 miles from north of Yosemite down to Cottonwood Pass and spreads on both sides of the crest, with an average width of about 20 miles. Between the peaks there are extensive highlands that are relatively flat and open. This is the land of the hiker and pack train, accessible only in summer."

The definition includes essentially all of Emigrant Wilderness, Hoover Wilderness, Ansel Adams Wilderness, John Muir Wilderness and the backcountry of Yosemite and Kings Canyon-Sequoia national parks. Although falling outside this strict definition, the glaciated, granitic area of the Marble Mountains and Trinity Alps further north, Desolation Wilderness near Tahoe, Mokelumne Wilderness, and Golden Trout Wilderness are similar. All of these areas are granitic and the trout habitat is similar. The strategies and tactics for taking trout covered in this book will apply throughout this terrain.

California's southerly extensions of the Cascade Range, Mounts Shasta and Lassen and their environs are forested and primarily volcanic. Their geology and ecology have more in common with Oregon than the Sierra Nevada and the following information may not apply.

*Prime habitat.*

*Early-season rainbow.*

## TROUT AND HABITAT

The lakes and streams of the High Sierra have the primary element of good trout habitat in abundance: cold, well-oxygenated, unpolluted water. Before 1860 there were no trout in the High Sierra except the golden trout of the Kern River drainage, and the Lahontan cutthroat in the headwaters of the Truckee, Carson and Walker rivers on the East Slope. Rainbows are native to the rivers and streams of the Central Valley and West Slope of the Sierra Nevada, but were held below 6000 feet by barrier falls. The high lakes were barren of trout, and so were the Owens Valley streams draining the Eastern Sierra south of the Bridgeport Summit. With the exception of the golden trout in the Kern River headwaters, the trout found in the High Sierra are the result of planting trout in the lakes and streams. The first plants were by the settlers and sheepherders who camped there. Later the U.S. Forest Service and California Department of Fish and Game planted trout in order to develop recreational fishing.

The principal trout of the High Sierra are brook, rainbow, brown and golden trout. Brook and rainbow by stint of planting are more numerous. Brown and golden are in the minority overall, although they may be in the majority in a given stream or lake basin. The Tuolumne River in Tuolumne Meadows in Yosemite National Park is an example of a stream where brown trout predominate. French Canyon Creek and Lakes in the John Muir Wilderness are an example of waters where goldens predominate. Although a native species, the Lahontan cutthroat trout is not present in the High Sierra, with the exception of a few lakes where it is planted and stream-resident fish near those lakes. Lahontan cutthroat are still found in waters draining the East Slope at elevations lower than the High Sierra, or in Pyramid Lake in Nevada. Although its common name is brook trout, brooks are classified scientifically with the trout-like char fishes.

Few of the 4000 or more lakes in the Sierra Nevada do not support at least some trout. The lakes that don't have trout are of two types—lakes that are subject to winter-kill and lakes without adequate spawning habitat. Winters are long and cold in the High Sierra. In winter-kill lakes, the snow pack is too dense to allow enough sunlight through the winter ice for photosynthesis. Without photosynthesis by plants, algae and plankton and the production of oxygen, which is its byproduct, the loss of oxygen through decay of organic matter in the ice-bound water will deplete the lake of oxygen if the winter lasts too long. In effect, the trout are smothered in their own lake. I have more than once found high lakes after ice-out with dead trout on the bottom.

Rainbow, golden, and brown trout must have clean, cold water running over stream gravel to reproduce. Brook trout can spawn in submerged gravel near underwater springs, and so can reproduce in some granite-bound lakes lacking inlet or outlet streams. Golden trout have managed a similar feat in a few lakes with gravel beaches having sufficient wave action to oxygenate the eggs. But generally trout can't survive for more than a few years if there is no inlet or outlet creek with gravel in which to dig nests and lay their eggs. Even if lakes without adequate spawning sites are stocked with trout, after a few years the trout are gradually caught by man, other predators, or die off, and the lake becomes barren again.

With either type of lake the choice is to keep planting every few years or let the lakes go back to being fishless the way they were in the past. Within the Yosemite and Sequoia-Kings Canyon national parks, the policy is to let these lakes go back to nature even if that means barren of trout. Elsewhere, while many lakes are still planted regularly, current policy is to avoid the expense of replanting a lake after a few plants have failed to establish a reproducing population of trout. As a result fewer lakes have trout than in the past when trout were planted in almost every lake and stream in the High Sierra. Older guide books may have out-of-date information about the presence of trout in a particular lake or stream as a result. See Chapter 12.

On the other hand, where the planted trout are self-sustaining, the happy consequence within a few years is a population of wild fish in both lakes and tributary creeks. There are numerous lakes and streams in the High Sierra with abundant, healthy and hard-hitting wild trout descended from trout planted as long ago as the 1870s. These are the clear, cold waters you want to fish.

## Basic Sierra Geology

The High Sierra trout habitat was created along with the mountains by four basic geologic processes: Tectonic motion, volcanic eruption, glacial reduction, and erosion. A collision of the Pacific and North American tectonic plates that make up the crust of the earth pushed up the rock mantle and formed the Sierra Nevada Mountains. A vast batholith was formed of molten rock forced up from below the earth's crust in the collision which cooled into

*Eastern Escarpment, Owens Valley.*

a plutonic blend of the minerals quartz and feldspar of varying concentration, known as granite, diorite, gabbro, and monzonite. The High Sierra is essentially a single massive composite block of granitic rock resulting from that tectonic collision.

A second collision, which occurred many eons later, pushed up the California Coastal Mountain Range and elevated the area known as the Central Valley above sea level, a process that created California. The collision also subducted or pushed down the western edge of the granitic block and sheared up the eastern side. The eroded top tilted west and became the gradual slope of the western side of the High Sierra which starts in foothills and rises to the high peaks. The east side, having been sheared up from bedrock, is much steeper. The High Sierra crest towers 7000-10,000 vertical feet over the Owens Valley, an image immortalized by Ansel Adams in his dramatic black and white photographs.

Since these tectonic events, later volcanic eruptions and explosions have added and destroyed peaks, and glaciation and erosion have carved and reshaped the rock, leaving lakes, valleys and canyons on both sides of the Sierra Nevada. In some areas mountains of dark older rock that escaped the granitic overflow co-exist side by side with lighter gray granite peaks and reddish lava cones. The High Sierra around Mammoth Mountain, which itself is a volcanic cinder cone, has these features. But, older peaks such as Mts. Banner and Ritter near Mammoth aside, almost all of the High Sierra is made of granite, especially the high crest south of the Minarets down to Mt. Whitney and beyond to the Domeland Wilderness.

There is good news and bad news as a result of this domination by granite. It provides great traction for hiking and makes a moonlight hike a thing of great beauty since it reflects the light. But it yields little in the way of dissolved minerals that can wash into the high lakes with rain and melting snow in the process of erosion. Minerals are essential in starting the food chain of plants, algae and plankton, that insects and small trout feed on, that bigger trout feed on in their turn.

Much of the High Sierra can be classified in the Hudsonian, and at very high elevation, Boreal, climate zones. In other words, the high elevation and low winter temperatures make the climate more like the sub-arctic than the rest of California. Only a few hundred feet of elevation gain on a trail can transition from the Canadian pine forest zone to the Hudsonian zone of stunted trees, tundra and bare rock. The growing season is short between snow-melt in early summer and the onset of the first snows in October. This is one reason there is typically so little total biomass or total living things in High Sierra lakes. The other reason has to do with the formation of lakes in the High Sierra.

## BASIC FISHING GEOLOGY: LAKES

The process of glaciation in the Ice Ages created the lakes of the High Sierra. They are of two basic types: grind-hollow lakes and moraine-dam lakes. Glaciers are formed from layers of snow that become compacted into ice as they are compressed over time. As glaciers expand or contract with changes in the amount of snowfall over tens of thousands of years, they grind down the rock underneath tons of snow and ice. This process creates, deepens and widens valleys, such as Yosemite Valley in Yosemite National Park, which was once filled with a river of glacial ice.

Under a glacier, the expansion and contraction grinds out depressions or hollows in the rock. Repeated expansion and contraction of ice in a hollow deepens it and creates sand and gravel. The hollow left in the bedrock forms a lake after the glacier melts. Vernon Lake in Yosemite National Park, which is essentially a depression in the granitic bedrock, is a good example of this type of lake. Moraine Ridge, which overlooks Vernon Lake, is an enormous pile of glacial debris left behind by the glacier that formed the lake, and the two are part of a grand scenic array of post-glacial geologic features. Even better, Vernon has good fishing for wild rainbow trout descended from an 1880s sheepherder's planting.

A moraine dam lake results when the glacier "retreats" or melts uphill toward the higher and thus colder end of a canyon during a warm era. As it melts, it releases the suspended boulders, rock, gravel and sand it ground out of the mountain when it was expanding during a cold era. If enough of this moraine is deposited in one area, it will form a dam across the canyon making a lake out of the melting glacier and later rain and snow. Convict Lake on the Eastern Slope is a good example of this type of lake. Fremont Lake near West Fork Walker River, where settlers once tried to drain the lake by ditching through the moraine dam to get their wagons past the upper end, appears to be the result of the effects of both geologic processes.

A variation of these processes important to fly-fishers results in step lakes. Where the glacier grinds out two, three or more hollows, or leaves moraine dams, and each forms at slightly higher elevations in the same canyon, the result is a chain of lakes. Often the lakes are interconnected by creeks. Variations in the habitat of

*The name of this lake rhymes with grind-hollow.*

*Whitebark pines near Mammoth Crest.*

at the lower end of the canyon. Three Island, Medley and Sandpiper lakes near the headwaters of Bear Creek in the John Muir Wilderness are a series of step lakes that typify this High Sierra habitat, with shorelines consisting of rock-studded tundra, a few winter-dwarfed trees, and plenty of golden trout.

At rock-bound lakes below treeline, water-loving trees typical of the sub-alpine High Sierra such as lodgepole pines or mountain hemlock will grow between boulders around the shoreline and even on bedrock, their roots clasped to cracks and crevices. The leaves, needles, twigs, logs and other organic waste from lakeside vegetation that enters the water become food for bacteria, diatoms, algae, insects that feed on such aquatic plants and animals, and insects that feed on such insects. This cycle builds up the basis of the food chain that supports trout. Lou Beverly Lake, which could be included as the lowest step lake with Sandpiper-Medley-Three Island in the lake chain mentioned above, is a good example of a "lodgepole lake" with many trout.

*Pine Creek Falls.*

each lake can result in a series of lakes where one or more of the lakes is barren, but other lakes have trout, or some lakes support one type of trout but not another. The highest lake might have goldens for example, the middle brook and the lower rainbow trout. Little Lakes Valley on Rock Creek on the East Slope contains an impressive multiple series of step lakes of both types and excellent fishing.

Lakes are also found in what are called basins, which are basically an area wider than a single canyon with a group or cluster of lakes and "tarns" or ponds. Characteristically basins are a relatively flat area where an ancient glacier left behind grind-hollow lakes, rimmed by a semi-circle of peaks, although often there are lakes in cirques on the flanks of the peaks. The Humphreys Basin in John Muir Wilderness, where golden trout can be found, is an example.

The key to this simplified geology is that the lakes are geologically recent and formed rapidly as the glaciers melted. There is little or no sedimentary overburden on the surrounding peaks and the rock resists erosion resulting in hard, rocky bottoms. Only a thin layer of silt and gravel ever settles into the granitic bowl of most High Sierra lakes. Such deep, slightly acidic lakes support little or no aquatic vegetation and dissolved nutrients are scarce.

As a rule, the highest rockbound Sierra lakes support only a few slow-growing trout. In other lakes at high elevation, there will be a turf (or tundra) of grass, sedges, wildflowers and dwarf brush around part of the shoreline. Turf is a good sign. It tends to indicate the lake will support more biomass and is likely to have good fishing. At lower elevation, the lakes may have a mix of turf, shrubs, and trees around the shore. A mix of turf and trees is an even better sign. It is common to find all three types in a step lake canyon: a high rockbound lake, a middle turf lake, and a turf and tree lake

## BASIC FISHING GEOLOGY: CREEKS

Creeks have some of the same characteristics as High Sierra lakes, since they drain the lakes and adjacent snowfields, eventually cutting deeper into the granite canyons carved by the glaciers, as they flow together into rivers. But creeks draining lakes and snowfields concentrate what minerals are present and are more likely to have vegetation along the banks at high elevation, even if it's only turf, than the lakes. As the creeks flow downhill, they accumulate organic matter and may support greater relative biomass than lakes above treeline.

The steep-gradient and rocky landscape makes for cascading, highly-oxygenated water. This is the habitat rainbow, golden and brook trout evolved in, and they thrive in High Sierra creeks and rivers. Brown trout do well in the creek environment but seem to be limited to water below about 9,000 feet, in my experience at least. But almost any creek connected to a lake supporting

*Carmine-splashed nugget of gold.*

trout will also have trout in the High Sierra. In fact, the fishing may be even better in the inlet or outlet creek than in many lakes. The lake is likely to have bigger fish, but you will often catch more fish in the creek.

The big drawback is that High Sierra creeks have seasonal low water and can even be dry late in the year or during a drought year, especially in the high-elevation headwaters of the creek. This means the number of trout can vary from year to year in the same creek or river. The habitat of a creek, especially a mountain creek, will vary. As a general rule, there will be better fishing where the creek flows over scattered boulders and small rocks and has both fast and slow sections of riffles and pools. A steep, talus-choked creek bed is not likely to be very productive, although it might have a few good trout in isolated pools. See Chapter 8.

But where the creek habitat is right, it can be really right. There are an astonishing number of trout in many High Sierra streams. I've reached over brush with my rod to fish pods of dozens of rainbows in pools on Falls Creek in Jack Main Canyon in Yosemite National Park, or had trout after trout hit a Lime Soft Hackle fly dead-drifted in Rush Creek near Mammoth, or had so many goldens rise to a Captain dry-fly-fished to the pocket water in Mono Creek near Silver Divide, the daunted fly was utterly worn out after less than an hour, the wings thrashed and the floss in tatters, to mention only a few examples. (These flies are covered in Chapter 10.) Until you have seen it, you simply won't believe the number of eager wild trout a stream can support cascading through the lithic High Sierra landscape.

How to fish the water draining this big rock block called the High Sierra is what the rest of this book is about.

*Hilgard Creek.*

*The high country trout, having learned from his harsh, sparse environment, will feed steadily on midges if that's all there is, but he'll also stop for a minute and grab a big caddis pupa that happens to swim by.*

*–John Gierach*

Most fly-fishing books that are not "literary" are aimed at skilled anglers. Many are meant for the spring-creek specialists. Spring creeks flow from a constant source of temperate water that supports a superabundance of prey species. Resident trout tend to feed on or "select" one species in a particular stage of development during a given day or even part of a day. To catch the trout you must figure out what the trout are feeding on, and select a fly that closely matches the size, shape, and coloration (in that order of importance) of the natural insect, since they will not take a fly that doesn't closely match whatever they have begun to feed on. Selective trout are merely trout that are temporarily conditioned (in the Pavlovian sense) to feeding on a single form of prey.

What "hatch" refers to in the phrase "match the hatch" is a developmental stage of an aquatic insect. At sexual maturity aquatic insects change from a crawling insect known as a larva or nymph that lives under water, to a winged insect that typically mates on the wing near the stream or lake. This change, known as metamorphosis, occurs within the exoskeleton or hard skin of the nymph which splits open across the back. The winged insect then crawls out of the nymphal skin or "shuck." This process is called emergence and the new insect is known as an emerger.

If this happens under water, the emerger swims up to the water's surface to fly off. This is typical of

*Bigelow sneezewood.*

caddisflies. In other species, the nymph first swims up near the surface before the exoskeleton splits, and the emerger, called a "dun," crawls onto the surface film of the water. In the exoskeleton, the folded wings are soft and moist; after the insect emerges, veins in the wings

*L Lake.*

fill with fluid and harden. Until the wings stiffen, the dun can't fly off, and trout will eagerly take the floating duns. This is typical of mayflies. In some species the nymph crawls out onto rocks, logs or aquatic vegetation, before the exoskeleton splits and the adult insect can come out. This is typical of damselflies and stoneflies. Thus success on spring creeks and similar waters involves deducing which stage of the life-cycle of the aquatic insects the trout are conditioned to feed on and selecting a fly to match.

In the High Sierra things are different. Because the environment is nutrient-poor, only rarely does one form of insect hatch in numbers sufficient for the trout to become selective. This situation does happen, typically in lakes in the sub-alpine Pine Belt (7500-8500-foot elevation), a few times a year for a few days when a particular insect is very abundant during a hatch. But this selectivity will last only so long as the insects are abundant, or not for long in the High Sierra.

A situation similar in effect to selective feeding occurs in lakes where the available food consists of only one or two insect types. These lakes are typically at higher elevation, where the only food may be zooplankton or midges. Obviously, fish that see only one or two food types in their lifetime have had no choice and will key on a fly that resembles what is available. Yet selectivity of any kind is an exception in the High Sierra.

Instead, trout in High Sierra streams and lakes forage ninety percent of the time, meaning they constantly search for and feed on a wide variety of insects as long as there is light to see the food in or on top of the water. In part, this is because, rare exceptions aside, the total biomass in the habitat is small and a few of several types of insect will be active. In small streams, fifty percent or more of the available insects will be terrestrials that hop, fly or fall into the water from streamside vegetation. In high-altitude lakes, the phenomenon of anabatic wind blows a variety of valley insects onto the water. See Chapter 7. This means the trout are presented with intermittent feeding opportunities on a small number of insects of differing size, shape and color throughout the day in High Sierra waters.

In streams, trout hold in a "pocket" (see Chapter 8) and try to eat any insect that floats, crawls, swims or falls into the water flowing past. In lakes, they swim around hunting prey. Although their diet is primarily insects, larger trout prey on smaller fish, frogs, even field mice that fall into lakes or streams. For these reasons an angler needn't worry about the "match-the-hatch"strategy in the High Sierra. It isn't necessary ninety percent of the time.

There are five basic types of flies for the High Sierra, or anywhere else for that matter. Two are dry flies that float on the surface, the backwing (or caddis) profile, and the upwing (or mayfly) profile. Two are fished under the water's surface, the larval (or nymph) shape and the pupal (or emerger or soft-hackle) shape. The fifth is the streamer, meant to imitate a minnow or other swimming aquatic creature, which is made with a longer hook and also fished under water. See Figure 1.

Since the trout are used to feeding on a few of several different types of insects, rather than conditioned to take only one abundant species—so-called attractor or searching patterns—the general-purpose flies that resemble insects by types rather than species work consistently. Although it may be necessary to try more than one size or color to get the fish to hit, one of these will work ninety percent of the time, without worrying about matching a hatch.

I can't say 100 percent because there are occasional days when the fish hit for a while, but stop, or don't hit at all, and nothing seems to work no matter what flies you try. This may be due to a weather change, a disturbance in the Force, or some other factor known only to trout, and it happens to every angler sooner or later, even in the High Sierra. On those days, hey, go climb a mountain, catch up on sleep, take a swim, relax with a book, or admire the many wildflowers—in other words, enjoy one of the many activities besides fishing that make trekking the High Sierras a lot of fun.

You have to think about what you are doing to fly-fish. The next chapter sets the facts straight about trout and will put you ahead of ninety percent of all anglers.

Figure 1. FIVE BASIC FLIES

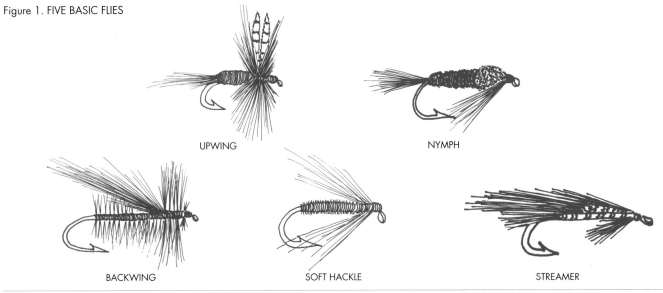

UPWING

NYMPH

BACKWING

SOFT HACKLE

STREAMER

# Chapter 3

# Beyond Myth and Lore: Basic Trout Science

*It is very easy to overestimate the intelligence of fish, but just as easy to underestimate his reaction time and the sharpness of his vision and other senses.*

*—Roderick Haig-Brown*

*Experienced anglers have a good understanding of trout habitat even if they do not think of it in technical terms. They know that trout are not randomly and equally distributed, so they do not cast a stream randomly.*

*—Robert Behnke*

There is a great deal of myth and lore repeated but little sense talked about trout. Altogether too much is written about insects in fly-fishing magazines and books, to the neglect of trout and their habits and biology. The cumulative effect is to create a false impression that precise imitation is essential. The true key to successful fly-fishing is simply to cast the fly where it will become visible to the trout in a natural way before you alert or "spook" the trout. This is known as correct presentation, and without it even the most exactingly tied imitation of an insect will be useless. By contrast, a mediocre fly or even the "wrong" fly, if well presented, will catch trout.

Correct presentation is not the same thing as fancy casting, although skill at casting helps. An angler learns to make a natural presentation from knowing about trout and their habits and using that knowledge. This doesn't mean you have to be a scientist to catch trout, although some very good anglers are wardens, biologists, foresters or rangers. Most fly-fishers acquire their knowledge from experience. But no matter how they learn it, what all successful trout anglers have in common is accurate information about trout. That's how they avoid wasting their time casting randomly in a lake or stream.

## TROUT SENSES

It pays to know how your quarry perceives the world. A trout's vision and other senses are different from a human's and very acute, as Roderick Haig-Brown pointed out long ago. That has important consequences for the angler. In fact, it is the basis for correct presentation of the fly as well as avoiding the single most common mistake anglers of all types make—the mistake of being seen or heard by the trout even before making a cast. Overhead movement, especially sudden movement, triggers avoidance behavior in trout. This is an instinct because many of a trout's predators, such as birds, attack from above the water surface. They also react adversely to sudden vibrations and sound transmitted through the water. To succeed, an angler has to learn first to avoid alerting the trout. Second, an angler has to learn to cast the fly where the trout will detect it. An angler that acquires these basic skills quickly begins to catch trout.

## TROUT VISION

A trout's vision is the sense most important to a fly-fisher, and arguably to the trout as well. Anatomically, a trout has an eye on each side of the skull connected to the visual lobes of its brain, which is set in the skull between the eyes. The visual lobes are the largest parts of a trout brain.

A trout's eye has a lens and retina, but unlike the eye of a mammal, a trout has a specialized muscle that allows it to focus by moving the lens in and out, like a camera lens. A trout's eye cannot dilate or regulate the amount of light passing in because a trout has no eye-lids and the cornea cannot dilate to adjust to the light. Trout eyes also have a reflective membrane, which collects and reflects light from objects in low-light conditions, such as dawn and dusk, and enhances night vision.

As the size of the visual lobes of its brain suggest, a trout has sharp vision within a range of at least 60 feet in clear High Sierra water. But a trout has binocular vision only directly forward and above the head, and is limited to monocular vision to the sides.

Trout eyes have both rod and cone cells, and they can perceive color very well, whether they realize it is "fly dubbing #7" or not. They can see light frequencies beyond the human visual range, something the manufacturer of fly dubbing #7 may or may not have taken into account in claiming it exactly matches the hatch.

## A LITTLE APPLIED FISH SCIENCE

There are at least five aspects of trout vision important to the angler. First is the so-called "cone of vision" of a trout. A trout swims in a world with a ceiling—the surface tension of the water where it lives. Because of its anatomy and the laws of physics governing light, a trout does not see above water in the panoramic way a backpacker sees the jagged Sierra peaks. Instead, a trout is limited to a "cone of vision" (also known as Snell's circle) within which it can see objects above the water surface. Beyond the edge of a clear circle over its head in the surface film, where a trout can see out, the rest of the water surface acts as an opaque mirror in daylight, reflecting the bottom of the lake or stream, and is dark at night. The mirror effect occurs because light hitting the water at an angle is reflected away.

*Hatchery rainbow.*

Despite the fact that this aspect of trout biology is well known scientifically, relatively few anglers appreciate its significance. The "textbook" aspects of trout vision are especially important to anglers fishing the extremely clear waters of the High Sierra. Visibility in the High Sierra is 20 to 50 times better than in silt, algae- and plankton-rich low-land lakes and streams, and the clear water allows a trout to make the most of its visual acuity.

Here's how it works. A trout sees above the water surface in a conical zone having a 97-degree arc. To get an idea of this, imagine walking around being able to see out only through a cheerleader's megaphone. (Go Bears!) Since trout see within a conical range, the deeper the trout, the wider the area it can see above water. The shallower the trout, the smaller the area in which it is able to see overhead. For example, a trout at 6-foot depth can see clearly above the water surface within a circle with a diameter of about 10 feet; at 3 feet deep can see above within a 5-foot circle; at 1 foot deep can see above within a 1.5-foot circle, and so on. See Figure 2.

What a trout sees outside this "cone of vision" is the lake or stream bottom reflected off the mirror of the underside of the surface layer. The cone effect limits a trout's range of above-water vision, but trout can see to the left, right, straight ahead and down. Trout can see a suspended insect in front of it as well as reflected off the surface layer mirror above it, for example. And, if you are thinking that means a trout has a better chance of seeing objects in the water than objects above it, you are right. Sub-surface flies such as a soft-hackle may be easier for a trout to detect than dry flies for that reason.

For the angler, the most important thing about a trout's cone of overhead vision is that it is constantly moving. As the trout swims around a lake, it is a sort of moving porthole in the ceiling. In a stream, where the

*Wild rainbow taken with a Foam Ant.*

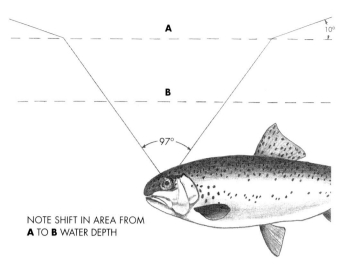

Figure 2. CONE OR (WINDOW) OF VISION

trout is likely to be holding in one spot, facing into the current, the water surface flows into and on past the cone in a matter of seconds. Thus a trout can see a fly on or near the surface only if it is cast where a trout will swim under it in a lake or drift on the current in a stream across the cone of vision. The second most important thing is the shallower a trout is swimming in a lake or holding in a stream the smaller the area of vision at the surface is, and thus the smaller the effective target zone is for casting.

Outside the cone of vision, an insect or fly on the surface is visible only as tiny, shiny dimples in the surface film mirror. If the water is roiled, as in a stream, or there are waves in a lake, the mirror surface will also be moving. The angle of the waves will create blind spots where light is reflected away from the trout (on the near under-side of the wave). Because the trout and the surface of the water may both be moving, the images the trout sees on or above the water in the cone of vision may be indistinct or distorted. That's good if the image is the fisherman, as the trout may be fooled, but bad if it's a dry fly since the trout may not be able to see it clearly unless it sinks under the surface film.

The second aspect of trout vision important to anglers is the effect of refraction. Light bends or refracts as it passes from air to water, and the reverse. This is also good and bad. Since the light bends (toward normal) when it hits the water, objects beyond the edges of the cone of vision are visible to the trout. They appear to be suspended above the water within the circle of vision. The wings of a dry fly can be seen by the trout before the fly actually crosses the edge of the circle, for example. If the angler can see the trout it will appear to be shallower than it actually is, because light bends in the opposite way (away from normal) passing from water to air. See Figure 3.

Because refraction reverses as light travels across a boundary between media with different refraction indexes (1 for air; 1.33 for water) a formula known as Snell's Law demonstrates the light hitting the water below 10 degrees is reflected away from the surface, and light

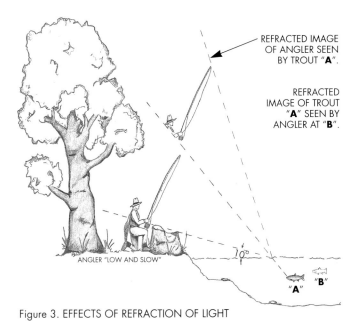

REFRACTED IMAGE OF ANGLER SEEN BY TROUT "A".

REFRACTED IMAGE OF TROUT "A" SEEN BY ANGLER AT "B".

ANGLER "LOW AND SLOW"

Figure 3. EFFECTS OF REFRACTION OF LIGHT

from the water hitting air at an angle below 15 degrees is reflected off the surface layer back into the water. That means a trout down in the lake can see light (images) hitting the water surface at 10 degrees or better, but an angler up on the bank can only see light (images) reflected back at greater than 15 degrees, giving a trout 5 degrees advantage. In practical terms, an angler walking up to the bank may be visible to the trout before the trout is visible to the angler because the image of the angler will be refracted up into the cone of vision before the image of the trout can appear in the angler's field of view.

The third aspect of trout vision important to anglers is that a trout cannot see backwards past an angle about equal to a line drawn from each eye to the tip of the pelvic fins. That leaves a blind area behind the tail where a trout can't see without turning its body. Obviously, a flycast behind a trout will not be seen. But more importantly, the angler is not visible to the trout when fishing from a position behind the trout. In stream fishing, this is the reason for the common advice to fish walking upstream. Trout face upstream into the flow of water to watch for prey drifting down to them. With a little knowledge of where in a stream trout will be found, an angler can "prospect" along, fishing upstream with reasonable confidence of not being seen and spooking the trout. See Chapter 8.

The fourth aspect of trout vision important to anglers is that a trout's eye is always open to the light. The human eye adjusts to light by narrowing the opening that lets light in to the retina. A trout cannot make that adjustment. A trout's eye is more adapted to gathering light for low-light conditions than dealing with bright light. This leads trout to leave the shallows and seek the depths of a lake as the sun rises in the sky. A not-so-obvious observation is that trout are more likely to be blinded by direct sun. Just as it's hard to see a baseball lost in the sun, a flycast where the sunlight is in the trout's eyes may not be seen. More than once I

*Mature golden trout.*

have seen a trout turn to take a flycast between the trout and dying sun in the late afternoon only after swimming past it, which changed the angle of light.

A trout has an even wider blind spot below and behind, under the tail, where it can't see. For this reason, small trout near the surface taking insects can be especially vulnerable to larger trout hunting from the bottom. This may be why the "across-and-down" presentation typical of streamer fishing, which doesn't get the fly very deep, is effective.

The fifth scientific aspect of trout vision is that a feeding trout orients to the area of binocular vision in front of and above its head. It is assumed this is because the trout sees two images of the prey (one in each brain lobe) and thus reacts faster to a double signal to its brain. On a stream this dictates the basic fly presentation of drifting or casting the fly into the cone of vision area above and in front of a trout. On a lake the area of binocular vision dictates casting into the area in front of and above the trout. If the trout are cruising near the surface in a lake, they orient to only a small, moving area on the surface along their path of travel. An angler must cast the fly not only near such a trout, but also in its direction of travel so that the trout will swim under or nearly under the fly. Otherwise, it will be outside the cone of vision and the trout is unlikely to ever see the fly.

## TROUT HEARING

The second most important trout sense to the angler is its hearing. A trout has ear-like organs, semicircular canals or bones containing otoliths (ear stones) which have annual growth rings. A trout's ear bones are fluid-filled loops lined with nerve endings. Movement of the fluid and ear stones stimulates the nerve endings and gives the trout a sense of movement and balance similar in function to human ear canals. Unlike humans, these are inner ears, located on each side of the brain, and not connected to the exterior. It is assumed that trout hear high-frequency vibrations with the inner ears.

But trout also have an extremely important sense organ that's unlike any human organ, known as the lateral line. The lateral line is a row of tubular cells on each side of its body, about midway between the back and belly, that leads from nerve tissue under the skin up between the lateral line scales, and out to the transparent outer layer of skin, that covers the scales. The lateral line is distinct and easily seen. The lateral line runs on each side of the trout from the tail to the head where it ends in several branches near each eye that penetrate the skull and are connected to the brain stem.

The tubular cells and the underlying nerve organ are filled with mucous. Low-frequency vibrations in surrounding water cause the mucous to "jelly jiggle" and

*The brightly colored fins of the brook trout are distinctive. In New England it was once common to use them for bait!*

stimulate nerve cells (neuromasts) under the skin, which send a signal to the brain. The nerves along the lateral line and lining the inner ear are the same type, and the inner ear-lateral line system is thought to work together. Thus it is fair to say trout "hear" waves, current, movement of other fish or insects, changes in atmospheric pressure, and other "vibes" in their watery environment with the lateral line. It is a sensitive organ with a range of about 30 feet.

Trout are believed to locate prey, such as minnows or even insects, by sensing even slight swimming vibrations. With that in mind, it's easy to understand why a trout can "hear" as well as see disturbances in the water, such as a poorly-cast fly line crashing onto the water and the thumps and bumps of an incautious angler tromping the streambank.

*Columbine.*

## Do Trout Suffer?

Besides the visual lobes, a trout's brain consists of two smaller olfactory (smell) lobes—pineal gland (sensitive to seasonal daylight), and a small cerebellum (mass of neural tissue) attached to the spinal cord. A trout does not have a cerebrum (frontal lobe) and therefore cannot think rationally or experience emotion. The parts needed are simply not there.

No doubt trout are sensitive to touch, but despite their sensory organs, they do not "experience" sensations of heat, cold or pain in the way sentient mammals do. Their bodies react to environmental changes metabolically and that may trigger behavior, such as avoiding warm, de-oxygenated water. Trout do not "think" about their environment. To be sure, trout resist capture, but that is as instinctive in trout as it is in all wild creatures. It is a mistake to say hooked trout "fight" since they aren't aware it's a contest and are only capable of an instinctive response to the resistance of the hook and line. It is equally a mistake to say fishing is cruel because trout suffer. The stress to the trout is metabolic not mental, whatever emotions may be felt by certain humans with "reservations" about fishing.

## Putting It All Together

From what you have read, you know you need to keep the way a trout perceives the world in mind to avoid detection and be able to present the fly effectively. A trout you can see may or may not have actually seen or heard you yet. There are likely to be numerous objects besides an angler in a trout's window. But it is capable of seeing or hearing you at any moment, and an angler has to be exceeding cautious to avoid alerting visible wild trout.

It is also important that the reverse (if you can't see the trout he can't see you) is not true. A trout is camouflaged in the water and is very hard to see against a deep-water background such as a lake. An angler silhouetted against the trout's horizon (stream bank or shoreline), wearing a red-checked shirt and boonie hat and waving a fly rod, is not hard to see. Recall that because of the effects of refraction, the angler or his rod or both will appear suspended over the water in the trout's cone of vision and may have been seen by the trout before the trout became visible to the angler.

The time of day (angle and intensity of light) are also important. The brighter the sunlight, the more objects tend to reflect light and the brighter the visible images become. The trout has the advantage, however, because the water diffuses and absorbs even bright light so that intense light will seldom highlight a trout. Fortunately for anglers, a trout is opaque no matter how well camouflaged and casts a shadow in direct light the angler can see, at least in shallow water with a pale bottom.

A trout's excellent vision dictates the strategy of wearing browns, tans, greens, blacks, grays and similar "earth" colors when fishing to blend better with the background, and its hearing dictates approaching the water walking slowly and softly. Avoiding sudden movements and keeping yourself and your rod low until you are ready to cast may be even more important. Keeping to shadows and keeping a screen of rock or brush behind you to blend into also helps to mask your presence from the trout. This can be summed up in an angler's mantra: Approach the water low and slow and from below the trout. "Below" is an aid to memory here, not literal for a fly fisher. It means approach from downstream or from cover when lakeside.

Chapters 7 and 8 cover the specifics of locating trout in lakes and streams in the High Sierra. But it can't be emphasized enough that an angler is wasting time casting where the fish can't see the fly. Unless it is cast where the trout will intercept it in a lake or where it will drift past a trout in a stream, there is no chance of success. That means casting with the trout's zone of binocular vision in mind, which means casting with the intent of presenting the fly above and in front of the trout.

## Debunking Some High Sierra Myths

There several myths out there about fishing in the High Sierra. The lore that goes with them is a sort of folk wisdom based on observations or impressions of fishermen built up over time. But often the myths or lore or both are inaccurate, or even plain wrong, as you will see.

**Myth:** Trout bite only at dawn and dusk.
**Lore:** The best fishing is at dawn and dusk.

**Trout Science:**
The myth is false, but there is something to the lore, since angler success can be greater in low light when the angler is harder to see. The origin of the myth is that stream-dwelling insects and minnows migrate or "drift"

*Foraging.*

at night. As it grows light at dawn, trout begin taking the stragglers, and as it becomes dark at dusk they begin taking the vanguard of the night's migration of insects. Some mayflies and caddisflies hatch in late evening which contributes to the idea. But in a lake, especially a high-altitude lake, the early and late idea isn't often true.

The vast majority of casual anglers are most active in July and August in North America. In low-elevation lakes, especially reservoirs subject to summer thermal stratification, the surface layer of water most accessible to anglers is cool enough for the trout to venture there to feed only in the early morning and late evening. Such lakes help create an impression the trout only hit twice a day. But if the angler can "get down to" the cool oxygenated water layer where the trout will be found, the fishing will be just as "hot" at noon at a foothill reservoir in 100-degree air temperatures as it was at dawn.

As a rule High Sierra lakes are cold year round and stratification is minimal. Trout will move out of shallows in bright sun, but even in shallows, the water temperature is not likely to ever exceed 60 degrees. That is well below the comfort level of trout, and a point easily confirmed if you venture a swim. Foraging trout will be hunting prey in a High Sierra lake regardless of time of day.

**Myth:** Trout are "starving" in spring, and go on a feeding "binge" and fatten up in fall just before winter.
**Lore:** The best fishing in alpine lakes is just after ice-out and in late season.

### Trout Science:
The myth and lore are half true. A trout's metabolism slows down in winter as water temperatures drop but trout still feed. There is no evidence trout "know" winter is approaching and fatten up, although changes in length of day may trigger fall spawning activity in brook and brown trout. What is true is that the growth and activity of the entire lacustrine biomass (all plants and animals in the lake) will slow dramatically in winter. As a result, just after ice-out, there are fewer insects available to trout and this forces the trout to actively forage to locate what is available.

In fall, the same conditions prevail but for a different reason. As a general matter, aquatic insect species will have completed their hatch cycles by October in the Sierra Nevada. The trout will also have been foraging for months. Predation by trout is significant in reducing insect populations in many high-elevation lakes. Lowland insects will also have completed their hatch cycles, so that the blow-in from anabatic winds drops off. See Chapter 7. Thus conditions similar to those of spring begin to prevail, where the trout must actively forage from a reduced food base.

Thus the lore is only partly correct since trout can feed in all seasons. But actively searching, hungry trout are more likely to try to eat a fly (fake insect) at ice-out or in late fall. There is an exception. Very early season hatches of midges exist in some lakes. Gary LaFontaine (a reliable observer) reports seeing midges using floating

*Sierra lily, a.k.a. tiger lily.*

ice in alpine lakes to emerge and trout taking them near the edges. I have not observed the midges, but can attest that trout hover under or near ice flows just after ice-out. I assumed they responded to it as structure, but maybe it was structure with lunch thrown in.

**Myth:** A guy named Seth Green created a strain of runty brook trout.
**Lore:** The Sierras are overrun with small brookies.

### Trout Science:
This myth is a well-known "fact" that just isn't true. Seth Green existed and was an early fish culturist in New York State in the 1800s. He started a private hatchery but was co-opted by the state when it started its own public hatchery system. But the idea that he created a runty strain of brook trout is nonsense. He started with wild trout and merely raised trout with genetic traits already present and dominant in the native trout.

According to the myth, brooks Seth created are capable of spawning at "unnaturally" early ages so that the trout breed after only one year and never grow large. That's true of brooks but not because of Seth. In New England and Appalachia, brook trout evolved in cold, clear and predominately small mountain streams. In that habitat, in which the rigors of winter and limited forage are dominant environmental factors, the genes for small early-maturing trout are favored because they are more likely to survive. The "window" for successful reproduction might be one mild winter out of three years. Trout taking three years to mature might miss the window and never successfully reproduce; trout maturing after one year would be able to reproduce, regardless of whether the mild year was the first, second or third winter. Thus early sexual maturity and short life-span were completely functional and adaptive traits in the brook trout's native range for millennia before Seth came on the scene. He is not the source of any "designer" trout.

---

There are present day exceptions to the 'small brookie' rule, notably the "coasters" of the Great Lakes, sea-run trout and Canadian trout inhabiting inter-lacustrine (between lakes) streams that reach 24 inches or more and over 5 pounds. These fish are races adapted to specific predator/minnow-prey relationships, where late sexual maturity and large size are adaptive. A giant race of Lahontan cutthroat trout once inhabited the Truckee River system, including Pyramid Lake and Lake Tahoe, based on a similar predator/prey relationship with the tui chub, that did not even reach sexual maturity before age 4. Age 4 is a ripe old age for most High Sierra rainbow, golden, and brook trout.

---

Size is a function of both available feed and longevity—more food over time equals larger fish. Thus early-maturing fish tend to be small, especially in a nutrient-poor environment, because they don't live long. And if spawning success is high, then such waters will be populated with many small short-lived fish. This is the reason, in many Sierra waters where they have become established, there are often many small and a few large brook.

Anyone familiar with the High Sierra or other alpine regions of the Far West knows this effect is not limited to brook trout. Golden and cutthroat trout exhibit the same tendencies to "overpopulate" lakes and streams with "runty" fish. That occurs for precisely the same reasons.

*Prime spawning habitat, East Fork Bear Creek.*

That is, like the native brook trout of New England, golden and cutthroat trout have evolved in small mountain streams and lakes where long, harsh winters and a short "growing season" favor early maturation. In habitats with good spawning, cold, clean water and few predators, goldens and cutthroats will rapidly expand in population to the carrying capacity of the food base. In the High Sierra, Lou Beverly Lake (mentioned elsewhere in this book) provides a good example. It has an abundance of quality spawning areas, fair food productivity and consequently is "over-run" with small golden trout.

Just the same, it is important to realize that from a small brook or golden's purely biological perspective this is a highly successful adaptation that guarantees their survival in the High Sierra. The vigor of these small wild fish and the stupor of the "snakes" (starving hatchery fish) found in planted lakes, attest to this truth.

**Myth:** There are no big trout in the high country.
**Lore:** A 14-inch fish is a big trout in the Sierras.

**Trout Science:**
The myth is false, but there is a lot of truth in the lore, since it is true of a majority of High Sierra lakes and streams. But there are also numerous waters that harbor trout of three to five pounds or greater in the High Sierra, as you can see from the back cover photo. The California record golden, a fish just under ten pounds, came from a High Sierra lake. In such waters an element of the equation for "runty" fish is missing.

It's really not that difficult: more food per trout = bigger trout. This can happen because there is simply so much food available that the trout grow to trophy size despite ideal spawning habitat, a condition prevailing in tailwater fisheries, such as the Tuolumne River below O'Shaughnessy Dam in Yosemite National Park. (Take care if you fish there; the rattlesnakes are also trophy size.) High productivity is uncommon in the High Sierra however.

Finding larger trout in the High Sierra is far more often a matter of finding those waters where the number of trout is low relative to the available food resources. These conditions are found in lakes with only limited spawning areas or none at all, that aren't planted, and with sufficient forage to support a few large trout. See Chapter 9.

The potential for taking a large trout from a High Sierra stream is limited because the water flow is typically too small by summer's end to support trout much bigger than 12 to 14 inches. That's not always the case and some streams do harbor trout over 20 inches, for example, the Kern River in the Kern Trench, South Fork San Joaquin above Florence Lake or Fish Creek. These streams have in common dependable water volume all season.

Having gotten a few facts straight, and knowing something about the quarry, what equipment do you need to catch High Sierra trout? The next chapter gets into gear.

# Chapter 4

# Some Gear Thinking: Rods, Reels, Lines & Leaders

*A five weight [rod] has enough backbone to punch a good sized fly into a breeze yet is still light enough to make gentle presentations and get a great fight out of pan sized trout.*

—Ralph Cutter

*T*here is no specialized fly-fishing equipment just for the mountains. But some gear is better suited to the needs of the High Sierra angler. If you already have fly-fishing gear, all you need to do is scale down the amount of gear you take, since it has to fit into a pack and be carried in. There is a long-standing debate between the "minimalist" and the "essentialist," the essentialist carrying many items the minimalist would consider adds-weight-to-the-pack frills. You may have to make a trip or two to figure out where your preferences fall.

## Fly Rods For The High Sierra

If you are a beginner, I recommend an 8-foot rod for the High Sierra. By far the most popular rod is a 9-footer. But it is my observation a beginning fly-caster can control the line a lot better with the shorter rod, and 8 feet is plenty of rod for learning to cast out to 40 feet or so. The shorter rod is also handy when fishing creeks and other small water, or brushy areas and under overhanging trees. See Chapter 5.

My experience is that four- or five-piece travel rods are the best choice. Although there is no reason you can't make the effort and carry a two-piece rod, I use four-piece rods for the High Sierra. Carrying a long metal rod tube around is a pain in the neck when backpacking, especially hiking off-trail, where you may need both hands from time to time. A four-piece rod packs down into a 30-inch rod tube which will fit inside an internal-frame pack or lash onto the frame of other packs. Modern multi-piece or travel rods simply do not deserve the prejudice against them. Modern travel rods are designed to be multi-piece, with integrated ferrule designs and a specific action or flex. The difference, if any, is a matter of degree and there is no reason not to go for the convenience of a travel rod.

Ideally then, you are seeking an 8- to 9-foot travel rod. A hard rod tube to protect the rod should come with it. A rod made for a 5- or 6-weight line is recommended if you have a choice. A 4-weight rod will work adequately, but as an angler gains casting proficiency, a 5- or 6-weight is more flexible in the High Sierra because the heavier line will cast more efficiently in windy conditions. My backpacking rods are all 5- or 5/6-weight.

I typically carry two rods into the High Sierra: my tried-and-true Fenwick Voyageur 8-foot four-piece and a medium-fast-action four-piece Lamiglas 9-foot rod, which I can fit into a single rod tube. I also have an 8-foot 3-inch Powell four-piece I sometimes alternate with these rods. The Fenwick dates from before the advent of graphite and is good-quality fiberglass; the others are graphite.

You don't have to have two rods but I like the security of having a backup rod, especially after watching a friend splinter the tip of an expensive rod against a boulder. The short rod is handy on small, brushy creeks and for close-in roll-casting (see Chapter 9), and the long rod for fishing lakes and on windy days. The Fenwick is also a sort of tradition in its own right. It was my second ever and first quality fly rod and has accounted for countless High Sierra trout since 1973. It's been my buddy on many a solo trip.

There is a lot of advertising hype about the action of rods. Graphite, depending on its modulus (dampening or resistence to quivering), can be constructed to have a fast, medium-fast, medium or soft action. Fast-action rods generate high line speeds and thus distance in the hands of an expert caster. But they demand exacting timing of the casting strokes and are harder to master. If you are less than expert, I recommend a medium-action rod. Softer-action rods are more "forgiving" of a beginner's casting mistakes and are the expert's choice for midging and small-stream fishing with small flies and light leaders.

**About assembling rods:**

What causes the ferrules to stick is most often dust and grit. Sticking can be prevented by making sure the male ferrule (the part that fits inside) of each section is clean before assembling the rod. A ferrule that persistently sticks can be treated with a tiny bit of silicon lubricant. A ferrule that is persistently loose can be treated with a little beeswax on the male section to help it stick. The hollow (or female) section can be cleaned with a folded pipe cleaner or similar tool.

## Reels

Choose a well-made single-action "click" drag reel. A precision-machined disc drag reel is simply overkill for the High Sierra, not to mention expensive. Camping is rough on finishes and fine tolerances, and there is an excellent chance of "dinging" the reel in the granite world of the High Sierra. Thrash a $350 reel on a rock and your trip will be less than pleasant.

Disk drag reels are overkill as a general matter in trout fishing. It wasn't so long ago that a reel was considered merely a place to store the line. A trout angler is seldom "into the backing" sufficiently to need a disc drag. In any case, there are several inexpensive and durable single-action reels on the market.

I carry two reels and a total of three spools all of the same make and model so that they are interchangeable. I carry two reels in case of damage to one, and three spools for three lines, matched to my rods. If I'm going ultra-light, say on a short trip, I'll sometimes carry only a reel and one spool loaded with floating line, and that's all you really need to get started.

## Lines

Lines have significantly benefitted from the "trickle down" effect of new technology. There are many "high-tech" lines now available, and several startup brands on the market are challenging the dominant line manufacturers. But what was top of the market technology a few years ago is now incorporated into the "economy" lines of the major manufacturers, and anglers have the benefit of excellent and inexpensive fly lines as a result.

As a practical matter, you will do most of your fishing with a floating line, even if you carry others along. But I also like the versatility of a sink-tip line for fishing certain structure in lakes. The three reels I carry contain, respectively, a floating weight-forward line, a double-taper floating line, and a medium-fast sink rate, 10-foot sink-tip. I use the double taper for fishing creeks and for fishing small flies over quiet waters and midging. A double taper also comes in handy for roll casting. See Chapter 9. A full-sinking line is worth considering in lieu of a sink-tip, if you plan to carry more than one line. There are a few lakes where getting a fly right on the bottom calls for a full-sinking line.

*Backpacker's tackle.*

## LEADERS

Even though 9-foot leaders are sort of a standard, I recommend 7 1/2-foot 4X tapered leaders if you are still mastering casting. It's easier to control the shorter leader. Seven-and-a-half-foot leaders work very well in the mountains, and you can always lengthen the leader. I prefer leaders with a line-to-leader loop already tied in. Bring at least four 4X tapered leaders, since attrition can be high in the back country and leader is essential.

In addition you will need a spool of both 4X and 6X tippet material. Clipping-off flies and re-tying knots quickly uses up the end of a tapered leader. I add ten inches of tippet to a new leader, to compensate for this,

and add more to rebuild the tip when needed. Tippet of 4X is about right for size 10 to 14 flies. I add a section of 6X with flies size 16 to 20, or to build a long leader in the field.

There are differences between brands in the hardness of the surface of monofilament tippet and leader. A

*Mt. Humphries.*

*Wild golden.*

hard-surfaced material can cut softer material when the two are knotted together. To help prevent this, choose tippet of the same brand and type as your leaders. Specialty leaders are not needed.

DEET (the insect repellant), stove fuel and some sun-screen products are enemies of fly-line coatings, leaders and tippets. They can attack the polymers chemically and make the material weak and brittle. The symptom is a series of "mysterious" break-offs, as your leader repeatedly fails whenever a trout takes the fly. The odor can't appeal to trout either. I take special precautions to avoid getting any of these materials on my flies or leader. Among other things, I prepare my leader and tie on the first fly in the morning before I put on any repellant or sunblock. I carry a supply of alcohol "wipe ups" to clean my fingers if I have to reapply repellant or sunblock during the day.

Leaders tend to coil when used right out of the package or if left on the reel for a while. On a sunny day this will be less of a problem since the leader will soften in the heat. But in the early morning it can be a prob-lem, creating obvious loops of line on the water after a cast. One way I deal with this, is to string up my rod, tie on my first fly, loop the leader and line around the reel frame, and back up to one of the line guides, where I hook the fly. I turn the reel handle enough to tighten the line and put a slight bend in the rod. I then set the rod aside while I make breakfast and get ready to go. The spring action of the bent rod helps stretch the leader and straighten out the coils.

## BACKPACKING WITH TACKLE

A four-piece rod in its tube is easy to haul. As mentioned, at about 30 inches it will fit into an internal-frame pack or stow secured to the frame of other packs. If the pack has "ski sleeves" the rod can be slipped under a side pocket. It can also be lashed upright to the back of the pack if it has compression straps or other lash points. I use mini bungee cords to secure rod tubes to the side of my pack. I prefer fabric-covered rod tubes for this since bungees, straps and other lashings grip the rough fabric better than a smooth metal tube, which can slide out. Use a double wrap at top and bottom around a metal tube lashed upright for that reason. Orient a rod tube with the cap up.

An advantage of stowing the rod on the outside of the pack, is that the rod is accessible if you stop on the way to fish likely water before reaching your destina-tion to camp. You can drop the pack and open up the tube to get at the rod, without removing it from the pack. I keep one reel, tippet and a box of flies handy in a side pocket.

Whether to carry a fishing vest is a matter of choice. I like using my shirt pockets and a fanny pack to tote my fishing gear when I'm not carrying my pack. A small box or two of flies, leader spools and leader clippers go into shirt flap pockets. More flies, extra leaders, spare reel, spools, lunch and my windbreaker go into the fanny pack. A quart of water hangs on my belt.

If I'm going ultra-light, I can get the essentials into a small, 2x4x6" belt pack. Both the fanny pack and the belt pack contain small "travel" tubes of insect repellant, sunblock cream and lip balm. The ultraviolet light at high altitude will quickly cause serious radiation burns (even of many darker complexions) if the skin and lips are left unprotected. I also carry a few pieces of hard candy, and a "blister kit." See Chapter 11.

I add a compass, pocket knife, water filter, wicking thermal undershirt, matches, a compact "emergency blanket," and an extra food bar or two to the fanny pack if I plan to day-hike any distance from camp. I take the consequences of a sudden change of weather or getting injured away from camp seriously when fishing in the High Sierra.

## FISHING LICENSE AND SEASON

If you are over age sixteen you are required to have a fishing license in California. They are widely available where ever sporting goods are sold, and at California Department of Fish and Game offices. Short-term licenses for out-of-state residents are available. You are required to display your license when fishing. This is usually done with a plastic holder pinned to your clothing or hat.

California fishing regulations apply and you are required to have a valid California fishing license when fishing in National Parks, National Forests and Wilderness Areas under the jurisdiction of the United States.

The basic season is from the last Saturday in April until November 15. Except for Inyo and Mono counties, the lakes and reservoirs in the High Sierra are open year around. Inyo and Mono county lakes are open during the special trout season for those counties. The general limit for trout in the High Sierra is five fish of any size and species per day and in possession. However, after you decide on a destination, you will need to consult the regulations since there may be special regulations that apply to a particular stream, section of stream, or lake. There is also a special 10-fish limit for brook trout that applies in certain waters of the High Sierra.

A free copy of the regulations is available when you obtain your license. The California Department of Fish and Game maintains a web site where you can obtain general information and the current cost of a license. You can research the regulations online at: http://www.dfg.ca.gov/fishing/fishregs.html.

*Camp at 11,300 feet.*

# Chapter 5

## The Rule of Three: Casting, Knots and Flies

*Trout fishing does not call for extra-long casts; in fact, usually an extra-long cast will work against the proper presentation of the fly. . . Instead of working for distance, the beginner should aim at perfecting his cast.*

*—Joe Brooks*

*T*his chapter assumes you are starting out in fly-fishing. If you already have some experience, you can safely skim through for information specific to the High Sierra. The Rule of Three refers to the three casts you need to know, three knots you need to know, and a fishing ditty I made up about flies: "One for the rock, one for the tree, and one for the little fishy."

## A Few Words About Fly Casting

Watch a fly-fishing video, TV show, or demonstration at an outdoor equipment show, and you're likely to see long casts with tight loops curling out dramatically, made with hi-vis lines. There are a few special situations where you actually need to make long casts like that, say steelheading on the Klamath or Yuba rivers. But don't let dramatic casting intimidate or impress you too much. More than eighty percent of all trout fishing is done within forty feet, often half that. Unless you plan to make casting a hobby, all you need to be able to do is cast well enough to fish. It's about fishing, not casting.

Joe Brooks was right. Any angler who can make a straight cast of twenty-five feet or so with a clean turnover of the fly has all the mechanical skill needed to fly-fish. Achieve that, and the ability to make longer casts will come naturally with experience fishing on the water.

You can get the idea but not the "hang" of flycasting from diagrams and reading. The only way to really learn it is to practice casting, and I highly recommend a lesson from an experienced fly-caster. The first resource, if you buy your rod, reel or line at a fly shop, is the owner or the staff. If the shop is worth patronizing, they will want to cultivate a consumer relationship with you, and will be willing to give you basic lessons. Ask about the lesson beforehand. If they are willing to sell you a rod or reel but refuse to teach you at least the basic forward cast, keep your money and shop elsewhere.

*The pause.*

## Rule of Three Casts: Forward, Side-to-side & Steeple

The forward cast is basic. Here are a few ideas that will help while learning to fly-cast. First, is to keep in mind the three basic elements of the overhead cast: (1) the backcast; (2) the pause to allow the line to straighten out behind; and (3) the forward or power stroke. "Visualizing" the line movements in the air both before beginning the cast and when executing the cast will help. But it is not all that difficult. Most people can learn the basic cast in an hour or less.

The common errors and frustrations of beginning fly-casters involve the timing of the steps of the cast. Not powering the backcast fails to impart enough energy for the line to fully straighten. Waiting too long before starting the forward stroke, causes the line to hit the ground behind. Tilting the rod too far back has the same effect. Not waiting long enough during the pause uses up the rod energy to reverse line still flying back, and causes the line to fall around the caster's head and shoulders on the forward stroke. Tilting the rod too far forward smacks the line into the water.

The other major error is thinking the power is in the caster's wrist. It is not. It is in the rod. This mistake leads to attempts to compensate by exaggerating the rod movements with the wrist, "whipping" the rod up and down. The correct arm movement is similar to a carpenter's swing with a framing hammer. A carpenter raises his hand and forearm together and draws the hammer down onto a nail, which uses the strength of the entire arm, not just the wrist. To get this, try pushing the rod back and forth while keeping the wrist "locked." This will force you to use your arm and help "nail" the overhead cast.

The line will sometimes "talk" to you and give you an idea what's going wrong. The most common message is a "pop" (or "crack" like a whip) behind you when you try to forward cast. This indicates you are pausing too long and the fly is dropping below the level of the rod tip on the backcast.

## False Casting

False casting gets separate treatment because many beginners acquire a false impression that it's necessary. False casting means to repeat the casting movements without allowing the fly to drop in order to lengthen the amount of line being cast. Watching a caster work out line creates the mis-impression that taking several strokes of the rod is the "right way" to cast.

If you can cast the distance needed to the target with one casting stroke then a skilled fly angler only makes one. If it only takes two, then a skilled angler only takes two, and so on. This helps avoid spooking trout with the line passing overhead or unnecessary flash from the rod. Even more important, you can only catch trout so long as the fly is on or under the water. A fly kept in the air with extra false casting can't catch anything except a tree.

## WILDERNESS CASTING

Fishing the High Sierra is fishing wilderness waters where there are no cleared "beats." It is rugged untamed country and the streams and lakes are often bounded by boulders, brush and trees that are obstacles to easy casting and a graveyard for flies. For that reason the other two essential casts are designed to modify the angler's backcast so that lake and stream areas with rock, brush and trees can be fished effectively. The first of these is the side-to-side cast.

## THE SIDE-TO-SIDE CAST

The side-to-side cast is performed essentially in the same way as an overhead cast, except the rod is held in the outstretched arm at a ninety-degree angle from vertical. The line is backcast parallel to the water (or lawn in practice) and forward cast parallel to the water. A typical setting, and the example here, is the narrow beach of a High Sierra lake, with small pines and shrubs crowding the shoreline, preventing the angler from completing a normal cast because of obstacles to a routine backcast.

To execute a side-to-side cast, step to the shore (real or imagined in practice) and turn in the direction you want to cast. Pull enough line off the reel and through the guides to begin the cast. Holding the rod level over the water, backcast parallel to the shore, with the casting arm extended over the water. With a minimum of false casting, work line into the air side-to-side as if making an overhead cast. Both the rod and line are kept over the water throughout the cast.

To cast in the opposite direction, the cast is executed with the rod held across the body. Stand at a slightly open angle to the water, to give the casting arm room to move in front of your chest. It sometimes takes a few tries to get the hang of it. The cross-body cast will seem especially awkward at first. Your arm and shoulder aren't as strong extended sideways; let the reserve power of the rod drive the line.

It is unlikely you can cast as far side-to-side as with a forward cast, since the line is held lower to the water. But with a side-to-side cast an angler can cover "impossible" near-shore water, especially brushy coves, and the water at the foot of cliffs, where there are rocky shelves, which are important habitat. Another typical setting would be standing on a shoreline boulder, with overhanging trees that leave no room for a backcast. With a side-to-side cast, you can reach near-shore risers and subsurface cruising lanes despite the foliage. See Chapter 7.

The side-to-side cast is also important when fishing creeks. Casting horizontally in the clearing over the middle of a small brushy creek will allow the angler to reach fish that can't be covered any other way. Even if the creek can be fished rock-hopping, a side-to-side cast can be used effectively to fish across bends and under overhanging branches to reach deeper lies while prospecting for the better trout. See Chapter 8.

*Glacier divide.*

*Mid-morning at the falls.*

## THE STEEPLE CAST

The side-to-side cast allows the angler to cast to water to either side of a brush-bound position on the shore, but what about straight out into the lake or across the creek? That's the utility of the steeple cast.

The steeple cast works by directing the backcast up and over the shoulder of the casting arm vertically (in the direction of a church steeple), and forward casting a partially open casting-loop. (If you know the clock method, this is casting 10 to 11:30 instead of 10 to 2 o'clock.) This is a fairly easy cast to learn once you know the overhead cast. The downside of the steeple cast is that wind gusts tend to push the line out of the intended direction of both the backcast and the forward cast.

The wind can also be your ally. If there is a breeze behind you, it will actually help this cast. Because you are backcasting against the wind, it will be easier to keep the backcast high and the wind will help keep it away from whatever is behind you. It will also help you to gain distance and shoot line. See Chapter 7, on Wind Dapping.

With practice you can cast fishing distances with a steeple cast. It is well worth practicing once you can forward cast. You will need to find a high, smooth wall to practice. You'll want a smooth wall since you are likely to be slapping it with the line a few times until you learn the timing. (The back wall of a shopping mall building after hours might work.) Stand ten feet or so from the wall, where there is room for the forward cast.

Facing away from the wall, but visualizing it behind you, try working out a short cast, stopping the rod with the tip pointed up and slightly behind the shoulder (the 11:30 clock position). Power the back stroke upwards rather than backwards, pause to allow the line to straighten "up" and forward cast. After a few attempts, you should begin to avoid hitting the wall, and complete the forward stroke with the line reasonably straight in front of you.

The setting where using the steeple cast is most important is the tree-bordered lake or creek where you would also need to use the side-to-side cast. Even if you find a peninsula or boulder to cast from, there may be trees behind you limiting the backcast, and forcing you into "back-to-the-wall" angling.

Sometimes what is behind you is not so tall as a tree or cliff. It may be low brush, a sloping hill or stream bank that threatens your backcast and fly. In that terrain, the backcast is kept as "steep" as needed to clear whatever is actually behind the angler. If you start by practicing with a wall behind you, then it becomes easy to learn to vary the height of your backcast, to work within the variable landscape of a wilderness.

# Rule of Three Knots: Surgeon's Knot, Surgeon's Loop and Improved Clinch Knot

There are many fishing knots. Like flies, there are plenty of opinions about knots, usually based on some negative experience when fishing a particular knot. But three easy knots are all you need to know to manage your leader and fly connections. These are the surgeon's knot for adding tippet to the leader, the surgeon's loop to make loop-to-loop connections, such as leader to fly line, and the improved clinch knot for attaching a fly to your leader. If you master these three knots, you might never need to know another fishing knot.

There are excellent alternatives, such as duncan (or uni-) knot, barrel knot and perfection loop. But they are harder to master. After teaching knots to a few folks, I feel the clinch and surgeon's knots are the easiest to learn. Knots, like casting, are best learned by practice. So, while I've included illustrations, you'll need to practice before you go if fishing knots aren't already familiar to you.

## Surgeon's Knot

The surgeon's knot is used to join two lines, most typically tippet to leader. It's necessary to know the surgeon's knot if you want to use some braided leaders. The surgeon's knot is basically a form of double overhand knot. It is tied by holding the two segments to be tied side-by-side, forming a loop, wrapping the tag ends twice around the loop, pulling the ends tight, and clipping off the excess. See Figure 2.

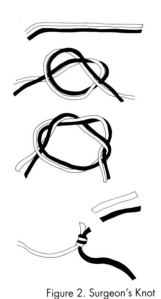

Figure 2. Surgeon's Knot

## Surgeon's Loop and Loop-to-Loop Connection

A surgeon's loop is a surgeon's knot tied with the same leader. To tie a surgeon's loop, double back the end of the line to be knotted. Pinching the doubled line in your fingers, form a loop and wrap it twice as in the above knot. With a finger, pencil or smooth twig in the loop, pull the tag and the loop in opposing directions to seat the knot. See Figure 3.

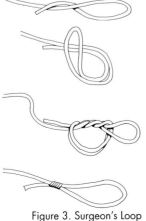

Figure 3. Surgeon's Loop

If you buy a fly line that doesn't already have an end loop, the fly shop can construct one which I highly recommend. A fly line will last for many years if well cared for and unless damaged an end loop connection need only be installed on a fly line once or twice even though you will use many leaders.

A loop-to-loop connection is used to attach the leader to the loop at the end of the fly line. The loop-to-loop connection is simple as shown in Figure 4. The only tricky part is that done right it makes a strong square knot and done wrong it makes a weak girth hitch.

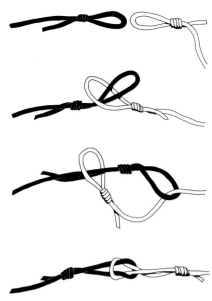

Figure 4. Loop-to-Loop

## Clinch Knot

The clinch knot is probably the most widely used fishing knot for attaching a fly to the tippet. There are three steps to tying a clinch knot, and one extra step to make it an "improved" clinch knot: 1) loop the leader through the eye of the hook; 2) wrap the tag end four times around the line; 3) bend the tag back and slip it between the eye of the hook and the first wrap. If you tighten the knot at this point—called "seating" a knot—it will make a fair knot.

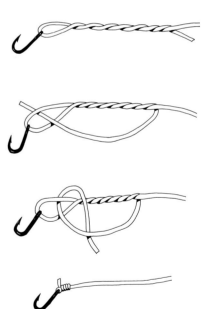

Figure 5. Clinch Knot

Take an extra step before seating the knot and (4) fold the tag end back between the tag and wraps. This improves the knot by binding the tag end down when the knot is seated, making it harder to pull apart. See Figure 5. Keeping the tag loose at Step 3 will help in Step 4. The most common mistake in tying the clinch knot is making too many wraps. It only takes four full wraps to make a strong clinch knot.

## Rule of Three Flies:
## One For The Rock, One For The Tree, One For The Little Fishy

That may be corny, but it's worth remembering. I hiked the Tahoe-Yosemite Trail many years ago. By the time I got to Benson Lake in Yosemite, I was practically out of food and completely out of flies. I ran into a summer ranger. He saw my rod and commented on the great fishing. I had to confess I hadn't tried it since I had lost all my flies to rocks and trees. He reached into a uniform pocket and pulled out a tiny box with two California Mosquitos, and gave them to me. I'll never forget and still thank the man. As a result of his generosity I was able to make a very welcome dinner that evening from a pair of stout rainbows cruising Benson's sandy beaches.

An angler learns to avoid losing flies as skill increases. But even after many years I sometimes concentrate too intently on the trout and forget the rocks or trees behind me and hang up my backcast. Sometimes I'm pushing the limits of casting room deliberately, trying to present a fly to a particular trout. Sometimes I'm pushing the limits, drifting a weighted nymph or bead head very deep near the rocks. But ultimately you will lose some flies if you fish aggressively. I made up the little ditty to remind myself why I bring a few of each fly.

While I've never seen any other fishing writer own up to hanging-up flies, there are some do's and don'ts about retrieving flies. First, stop the cast if you feel the fly hang-up. If it's caught on a tree branch, the branch is likely to give a little and there's a good chance the fly won't snap off. A pine bough is mostly needles, and a fly will pull loose from needles. Don't use the rod to try to pull down a fly. Grasp the line and tug gently and see if the fly pulls loose. What often causes a fly to snag on a tree is the fly whipping around a twig, rather than the hook actually sticking into anything.

*Ripe gooseberries.*

*The start of the journey from sky to sea.*

If you hang-up in brush or a tree you can reach, simply lower your rod to the ground and follow the line and leader back to the fly and untangle it. If it's out of reach, draw the leader tight in your hand, especially if you can see the fly dangling, and gently pull to see if you can get the fly to whip in reverse and pull free. If that doesn't work, or the hook snags the twig as it spins, check to see if you can reach the limb to pull it down. Many branches and small trees are limber and may bend far enough to allow you to reach the fly.

Keep the leader loose in your hand if you try this, however, since the limb may spring back and you will snap off the fly if the leader is taut in your grip. If a few attempts convince you it's snagged and it's high out of reach, grip the leader and snap off the fly with a sharp tug. A steady pull is wrong since it will stretch the leader and weaken it. Clip off the end of the broken tippet and even add a little fresh tippet if necessary to be sure your next knot is strong.

The fly is far more likely to snap off on a dropped backcast that clips low brush or rocks behind the angler. Usually you can hear the snap. If that occurs, don't stop casting, instead complete a false cast and let the line fall behind you in the direction you lost the fly. Turn and lower the rod and follow the line back. It may lead you to the object that caught the fly. If this is a shrub or low tree, you may find your fly hanging there or caught in a leaf or twig. I've sometimes been able to turn and see the branch still quivering.

The success rate for recovering flies lost on a backcast is only fair. As you will quickly discover, a fly is mighty small and difficult to see when you start searching even a tiny part of the wilderness. You will still have to bring "one for the rock, one for the tree, one for the little fishy" and maybe even stash an extra Mosquito or two somewhere in your pack.

Having gotten to the point of being rigged and ready, what about fishing? The next chapter is the first angling lesson.

# Chapter 6

# Angler Ethics:
# Hooking, Playing and
# Releasing Trout Unharmed

*And if a trout is taken, and killed, its colors and even its form fade so quickly that the beholding is momentary only, the vision as ephemeral as the final splendid minutes of a sunset. One can gather the most delicate of the spring wildflowers, but cannot collect these brilliant bits of living water.*

–David Carroll

*Improper handling probably kills the majority of trout. . . Handling time can be greatly reduced if you use barbless hooks.*

–Ralph Cutter

*T*he debate is over: there is now scientific confirmation trout survive catch-and-release angling. In this chapter I explain how it's done correctly. Catch-and-release is an ethical practice and I encourage you to adopt it.

Catch-and-release has practical aspects as well as an ethical aspect. As your skill level rises you will catch many trout throughout a day of fishing, and many of them will be small—6 to 8 inches or so. Even if you plan to keep a few trout to eat, you will need to limit your kill.

## FOUR PRACTICAL REASONS FOR CATCH AND RELEASE

First, it is illegal to take more than five trout per day in the High Sierra, except in certain waters where ten brook trout under 10 inches may be taken. Many anglers prefer to keep the bigger fish and put the small ones back. You should know, however, that skilled anglers, if they keep trout at all, will only take a few of the "pan-sized" trout caught to make a meal. They leave the larger trout to be caught again another day and to spawn—so their genes remain in the pool.

Second, as a general matter there is no way to preserve dead trout in the High Sierra. If you are fishing very far from your camp, you will have the problem of transporting fish meat back and then keeping it fresh once you are back in camp. Third, campfires are prohibited in most areas so you either have to pack the extra weight of a frypan or plan on making trout boiled over a camp stove palatable. And fourth, but by no means least, trace odors of cooked trout on your clothing and cooking gear, not to mention bones tossed into a fire, can be a savory beacon to marauding bears. They might try to locate the source of the scent of fish on your t-shirt, even if you are wearing it in your sleeping bag at 2 a.m.

Because of these ethical and practical reasons you need to know how to catch-and-release fish with a minimum of harm. Learning to do it right is the first angling lesson.

## HOOKING FISH: BE ALERT, PREPARED AND QUICK

Hooking trout after they take a fly is not a simple matter. Despite their sharp senses, trout sample a lot of non-food items. They can quickly spit out what doesn't feel right. An angler needs to be alert, prepared and quick to set the hook when a trout takes the fly.

## BEING ALERT

Alert means to be aware of where your fly is after the cast in order to see or feel a fish take it. Fishing a dry fly requires following its drift in a stream. It takes a little practice to see it as it drifts along in the riffles of a mountain creek. Keeping an eye on a dry fly is easier but especially important on a lake. In a stream the current helps to set the hook when a trout tries to swim away with a fly. But at a lake the water is still or nearly so and the angler has to set the hook in the brief moment before the trout rejects the fly.

The fly is seldom visible when using a wet fly or nymph. The angler must keep an eye on the line and watch for any hesitation in its movement, which may signal a trout has taken the fly. The lack of direct visual clues makes nymphing more difficult to learn. It's easier to see the trout or its splash as it strikes a dry fly than to detect the more subtle line movement that gives away a trout taking a nymph. A colored strike indicator attached to the leader above a nymph is useful because it will bob or twitch if a trout takes the fly.

## BEING PREPARED

To be prepared, keep track of the fly line. A little slack in the leader is OK, but extra fly line on the water is not. Extra line on the water must be pulled in or lifted off the water before there is any effect on the fly. In that brief moment of delay a trout can spit out the fly. There should be as straight a line between the rod tip and the fly as practical, unless you are deliberately mending line. See Chapter 9.

Be mindful of line stripped off the reel. Loose line draped over rocks or brush inevitably snags. It is best kept in coils at—but not under—the angler's feet.

## BEING QUICK

React as fast as possible when the trout hits the fly. Be quick but don't rear back on the line. Enough pressure to penetrate the jaw tissue is what's needed. I find it best to use what I call the "third haul" (after the double haul cast) to set the hook. This is a coordinated movement: lift the rod high with one hand while gripping and pulling line down through the line guides with the other. This both tightens the line and lifts it off the water, so that there is a direct straight-line pull from the rod tip to the hook.

*J. Hall, alert and prepared.*

Sometimes a trout will take a fly and swim off with it, making hooking relatively simple so long as the line is pulled tight before the fly is rejected by the trout. Other times, in the clear water of the High Sierra, the angler will be able to see the trout coming for the fly. There is a tendency as a result to try to set the hook too soon and pull the fly away from the trout. The best cure for this is to watch for the flash of white as the trout opens its jaws. Since inside of the mouth is white, it makes a visible flash in the water. Pause for an instant after the white flash is seen, and then set the hook. That pause allows the trout to take the fly into its mouth where the hook has a chance to penetrate the jaw.

# PLAYING A FISH:
# FOUR RULES OF SUCCESS

In the bad old days, it was considered something of a feat to catch big fish on very light leaders, which meant playing the fish (letting it swim around and tug the line) until exhausted. This took skill but it also tended to kill the trout. After a few minutes the effort of resisting the line will cause a build-up of lactic-acid in the trout's muscles, the same metabolic effect that causes "burn" and cramps in human muscles during exertion.

A trout played out to the point of complete exhaustion will go into metabolic shock even if put back into the water. Add to that being lifted out of the water where it cannot breathe and you can see how it's tough on the trout. The net effect is something like tackling a runner who has just crossed the finish line of a 10k foot race, and holding his head under water.

Keeping these effects on the trout in mind, the basic principle of playing trout in catch-and-release angling is easy to see: Play the trout as little as needed. Small trout are the easiest to catch but suffer the most from hooking. That dictates pulling small trout in rapidly and not trying to play them at all.

Mid-size trout can withstand the rigors of being caught better than small trout. But they should be played as hard and fast as you can without breaking the leader. Modern leaders are pretty tough stuff; 5X leaders will take three pounds or more pressure, 4X five pounds, before breaking. So even fish in the 12- to 14-inch class should be pulled in with a minimum of play, since there is little risk the trout will break the leader.

Larger trout pose different problems. The idea, after all, is to bring the trout to hand before release. If you try to force a big trout to shore (called "horsing" the trout), it is likely to break the leader or throw the hook as it leaps and tugs and shakes its head. Thus keeping the trout hooked until you can land it becomes a problem with bigger trout.

**First Rule:** Rod Tip Up
The first rule of playing a fish is to keep the rod tip high. The drag of the line in the water adds substantially to the pressure on the leader. Keeping the rod tip high keeps more line out of the water and reduces this pressure. It also helps to keep the line out of brush and the leader above any rocks as the fish struggles against the hook.

**Second Rule:** No Slack Line
The second rule is to keep the line tight and avoid slack. Slack in the line is why most fish are lost. A tight line pulls against the hook and keeps it embedded in the fish's jaw. When the line goes slack, the trout has an opportunity to twist itself off the hook.

**Third Rule:** Trout Jumps, Tip Drops
The third rule is to drop the rod tip when a trout leaps. As the trout leaps up, it drags line with it into the air, increasing the pressure against the leader. Dropping the rod tip creates a little slack to absorb the pull on the line as the trout drops back into the water. But leaping also allows the trout to shake against a slack leader while it's in the air, increasing the trout's chances of throwing the hook. For that reason, it's important to get the rod tip back up as soon as the trout is back in the water, in order to keep the line tight and the pressure on the hook to keep it in the fish's jaw.

**Fourth Rule:** Side Pull Turns Trout
A fourth rule is to control the direction the fish runs by pulling its head to the side. There are times when an angler needs to control the fish even though it is still "hot" and fighting hard. A fish may be running toward logs, weeds or rocks where the line can get snagged or break off. To prevent this and "steer" the trout away from such hazards, the rod tip should be held sideways and parallel to the water's surface. A steady sideways pull to the left or right will force its head to turn to the side, and the fish will change direction and follow the pull.

# RELEASING FISH UNHARMED

The most important rule after the fish is brought to shore is: Handle the fish as little as possible. Mishandling fish can cause serious injury.

Barbless hooks are highly recommended since they hold better than a barbed hook (because they penetrate deeper) and are easier to remove, enhancing trout survival after release. If you are using barbless hooks, it is easy to unhook a small trout and avoid touching the fish. This is done by sliding your hand down the leader to the hook, lifting the trout with the hook and shaking it off over the water.

If you have to handle the fish, wet your hands first. A fish is covered with mucous or slime that acts as a protective barrier. The slime will stick to your dry hands and fingers. The lost mucous will eventually be replaced, but while it's regenerating, the trout is open to attack by disease and parasites that the slime protects against. Many trout have been found with fungus growing on their sides in a finger pattern.

If you have to hold the fish to unhook it, try to grip the lower jaw between thumb and forefinger. Be careful with small trout since you can crack the cartilage. Use the other hand to back the hook out, pushing with the thumb against the eye of the hook. Small forceps (stocked by many fly shops) are handy for gripping the fly, especially if the trout is hooked in the tongue or throat.

If the fish is hooked near the gills, or is bleeding, it is probably best to avoid removing the hook. Simply cut off the leader and forget the fly. The trout has digestive enzymes that will rapidly dissolve bronzed hooks. Avoiding further injury gives the trout a better chance to survive.

Never touch the gills. Touching the gills ruptures the tiny capillary arteries and causes a fatal injury. Try not to grab the trout around the belly. If it squirms you are likely to squeeze to hold on to him and that can cause injury to the internal organs. You may have noticed that the big fish photos in fishing magazines now show the fish being held with one hand under the head and the other on the caudal peduncle. This grip avoids injury to the internal organs. See back cover.

## REVIVING A PLAYED-OUT FISH

The small wild trout of the High Sierra are so vigorous that if you land small fish quickly you will seldom have to worry about reviving them. They will dart away as soon as you return them to the water. If you have had to play out a larger fish, or have kept any trout out of water for more than a minute to remove the hook (and maybe take a photo), it may not recover. A trout in shock will sink and roll onto its side or belly when you put it back into the water. You can watch for a few seconds to see if the gills are working and whether it swims off. But if the fish doesn't right itself and start swimming you need to revive it.

Making this judgment takes some experience, and if in doubt it is clearly better to err on the side of taking time to revive a fish. If you are on a stream or over deep water, the fish may drift out of reach before you realize it needs help to recover. On the other hand, the fish will quickly let you know by struggling to get away if it doesn't need help.

The way to revive a fish is to hold it upright under water, with your hand under the belly of a smaller fish or by the tail of a larger fish, and move the fish back and forth to get water to the gills. It should respond fairly quickly by starting to work its gill plates. Stop periodically to be sure it's the fish moving its gills. Note that the mouth needs to open on the forward stroke to get the water to pass over the gills. If the gill action stops when you stop, keep moving the fish until you feel it start to move in your hand. As it revives the trout will try to swim off, sometimes before it is really recovered. Try releasing it but if it sinks and rolls it is not ready and needs more time in hand.

With larger fish that have been played out and stopped struggling, simply sloshing back and forth may not be enough to get the water flowing over the gills. Grip the fish by the lower jaw with your thumb and forefinger to force the mouth open. Hold it under water and jig it up and down to force the jaws to hinge open and shut and force the water over the gills. Be gentle so the

*This grip avoids risks of handling.*

trout isn't injured and your fingers aren't lacerated by its teeth. This is not a good idea with smaller trout since it is too likely to damage the jaw. But it will get a bigger fish up and going much faster than simply swishing it back and forth.

It goes without saying that an angler should avoid allowing the fish to flop against the bank or shore-line gravel and rocks when landing it and avoid dropping the fish anywhere other than into the water. Many trout can be lifted with the rod up over the shoreline and into the hand where they can be unhooked. But if the trout is of any size or is still "hot" it may be hard to handle as it continues to flip and squirm. This is a danger point since the angler may lose his or her grip on the trout and drop it onto rocks or gravel. It's far better to try to keep the fish in or over the water when removing the hook.

When casting from shore it is a good idea to plan where to land your fish before you cast. If you are fishing a rock-bound lake or bedrock stream, you may be fishing from boulders or ledges several feet above the water's surface. I haven't had much success lifting fish bigger than 8 inches or so more than three feet with the rod. The fish tend to break off and fall onto the rocks before flipping back to the water. What is needed is a spot where you can get down to the water and work the fish in, keeping it in the water as much as possible before release. I plan a route down to the water ahead of time if I cast from an elevated position, and I pass up an area where I can't get down to the water to play and release a fish.

With casting and how to release the trout in mind, catching trout is next in order. The next three chapters explain how it's done in the High Sierra.

# Chapter 7

# On Dawn Patrol:
# How to Fish a
# High Sierra Lake

*Alpine-lake trout often cruise shallow water along more-or-less regular routes, sometimes alone, sometimes in small, loosely organized packs.*

*—John Shewey*

*Fish often cruise established routes; once you determine those routes, you know where to work your flies when spotting conditions deteriorate.*

*—Rich Osthoff*

## ANATOMY OF A HIGH SIERRA LAKE

High Sierra lakes are predominately granite-bound. Although each lake has unique features, Sierra lakes break down into two basic profiles. One, typical of cirque or high under-the-peak lakes, consists of a granite gully filled with water having shallows near the outlet and a steep deep drop-off under cliffs or talus at the other end. Any wind-dwarfed trees and shrubs will be concentrated around the outlet. The other, typical of turf lakes and sub-alpine lakes ringed by trees, is a hollow in the bedrock with a narrow band of shoreline shallows and one or more deeper areas. Both types will have "structure" consisting of granite peninsulas, shoreline boulders, islands, submerged boulders, bedrock ridges and shelves, and if there are trees, fallen logs. The edges of drop-offs, aquatic plants, gravel beaches, inlets and outlets and the shoreline itself are also structure.

Thin patches of silt and gravel over solid granite and scattered boulders compose the bottom; tumbled rocks are characteristic of the shoreline of such lakes. The lack of suspended particles or organic matter makes the water extremely clear. With polarized sunglasses the bottom and bottom structure will be clearly visible out to a depth of

*Golden cruising.*

thirty feet or more. It can be hard to judge depth and the size of objects in the clear water. The clarity of the water is negative in that it makes the angler more visible to the trout, but positive in that it also makes prey more visible

*Shoreline structure.*

*The angler's friend.*

to the trout, and the trout more visible to the angler. The clarity of the water and the topography of the lake bottom dictate the basic strategy for fishing High Sierra lakes: Sight-casting to trout cruising near structure.

The most important structure is the shallow shoreline. Not only is it accessible, but in the "sterile" lakes of the High Sierra, which have few nutrients and limited aquatic life, the shoreline is where trout search for food. Shoreline shallows get the most sunlight and are more likely to have aquatic plants and organic debris such as submerged logs, where insects using them for food or shelter are found. This attracts trout despite the lack of cover in shallow water. Bouldered shorelines that drop off into deep water provide trout cover in the deeper water. As an example, an angler can expect to locate fish along the drop-off to deeper water near a shallow shoreline cove between bouldered points of land, especially if the cove has aquatic plants and a drowned log or two to enrich the habitat.

## THE ANGLER'S FRIEND: ANABATIC WINDS

Wind is a constant factor in the High Sierra, especially in late summer when most people visit. The temperature extremes between the hot, humid San Joaquin Valley or dry, hot Owens Valley, and the cool high-altitude air causes winds both afternoon and evening. I'd say they are more pronounced in the afternoon. A breeze is both

enemy and ally of the angler. Fly-casting takes extra effort after the wind shifts onshore. But it is your ally because the wind causes a surface current (in the direction of the waves) that the trout face into as if they were in a stream, and it concentrates flotsam against the windward shoreline or along current edges known as wind seams or foam lines. This includes insects from the lake such as drowned emergers and spent spinners, terrestrials knocked out of shoreline shrubs or trees and the all-important blow-in.

*Shoreline structure.*

*Rainbow and suncups.*

Blow-in results from thermal gusts or updrafts from the hot valleys that flow up and over the High Sierra, called "anabatic winds" by meteorologists. When the drafts cool and the air stops rising, anything borne on it starts to fall, including insects. This causes a more-or-less daily 'rain' of insects to drop onto the lake surface during summer. Since the sources of the insects are the valleys and foothills, the insects tend to be flying terrestrial insects such as beetles, leafhoppers or moths, and small insects, mostly ants, likely to be caught up in the wind.

Since they are terrestrial, such insects are not buoyant for long, assuming they are still alive when they hit the water. They drift on the surface with the wind current and after they sink, drift in the top two to five feet of water. The trout cruise this surface zone picking off the insects that have dropped in. This zone can include most of the lake and cause the trout to spread out, but the blow-in can also fall onto only one part of the lake and concentrate trout there. Any cross-wind will push the drifting insects along and they will collect against the windward shore or along wind seams and foam lines, where the trout will also cruise to feed.

The wind typically dies down in the late afternoon, at least for a while, before the evening breeze starts up. The evening breeze results from a reversal of the temperature difference between valley and mountains, as the lowlands start to cool at the end of the day. During this afternoon calm, before the atmospheric change, if the lake has insects ready to hatch, they may start to rise. Sometimes these are caddis, but more likely in the High Sierra, they will be midges. Midges are small (tied on size 16-24 hooks) and their larvae dwell in bottom mud and silt. Because mud and silt are relatively scarce in granitic High Sierra lakes, in my experience the hatch will tend to be concentrated in one or two spots around the lake over areas where the silt has settled. Fishing midges is covered in more detail in Chapter 9.

It may not start until eight p.m. or so, but sooner or later an evening breeze will begin. This breeze creates another surface current that captures and carries insects from the evening rise in the direction of the waves toward the windward shore. It will likely be too dark to fish by the time the wind stacks the insects onshore, but the morning will be a different story.

## DAWN PATROL

Because the water is chilly, and it takes a while for the shallows to warm after the sun rises, mid-morning can be the most productive time of the day for fishing a High Sierra lake. The trout patrol the shoreline and edges of the shallows, searching for prey and the leftovers from the blow-in and evening rise of the day before, concentrated by the wind along the windward shore or around any above-surface structure such as an island or peninsula, the lee behind it and rocks and logs along the shore. The base of cliffs and even snow banks and drowned shrubs will collect wind-drifted debris and insects along their waterline. The trout cruise along hunting for these leftovers, often within inches of the shore or other structure, and in water merely inches deep.

Many, many times I have watched such a cruiser work steadily along the shoreline, rising here and there, one foot, then two feet, then six feet, then one foot again from the shore line, picking off insects in the surface film. Sometimes even very large trout will brush against the rocks or grass onshore, hunting insects washed up the night before. Many times I have observed the trout cruising in a circuit along the windward shore a few feet out, weaving in and out of the shoreline structure, or along a drop-off parallel to the shore, patrolling for the leftovers. I call this feeding activity the "Dawn Patrol."

## DAWN SHADOW

The light can be the angler's ally in the morning. There will be a shadow on the easterly side of the lake, caused by cliffs, trees or the peak or ridge above the lake that blocks the light from the rising sun. That area of shoreline will be out of direct sunlight for a period of time, an hour or maybe two hours depending on topography, while the lake is gradually subjected to direct light from the rising sun. The angle of the light masks the presence of the angler on shore and reflects back from the bottom—you can see the trout or their shadows across the bottom, but you will be hard to see if you are careful and stay back and fish from within the dawn shadow. This effect gives the angler a rare visual advantage over the trout.

*Dawn shadow, Lamark Lake.*

# FISHING THE DAWN PATROL

To ace the dawn patrol, you lead the trout as they cruise along by casting ahead of them. Use a small dry fly to start with. When you spot a rise, watch for a second or third rise to indicate the fish's direction. Cast to a spot in the trout's direction of travel but not closer than about ten feet to the last rise. Give him time to approach. If there is a rise near the fly, or when you are sure the trout is close, twitch it once and the trout should hit the fly. I recommend a dry fly or a soft-hackle fishing within ten feet or so of the shore, or if casting next to submerged structure. A nymph tends to sink as you pause for the trout to swim toward it and can snag shallow structure.

Sometimes a rise won't be repeated in a way that indicates a direction, or may be fairly close to you. If that happens, cast directly to the area of the last rise. If you are quick and accurate, it is deadly to cast into the "ring of the rise," the circular ripple caused by the trout taking a surface insect. It has been suggested the trout "instinctively" hits the fly-fished this way. Whether that's true or not, it may be the only practical tactic if you can't judge the direction the trout is patrolling.

### More about refraction:

Refraction is important in the clear water of Sierra lakes where you can often see the trout at a distance. Neither the trout nor underwater structure is quite where it appears to be. A trout will appear to be shallower than it really is. Casting ahead of where the trout appears to be as it approaches will place the fly above its true position in the cone of vision, and leading a cruising trout "too much" is a good idea if you want the trout to swim under the fly.

After a while, as the light increases, the trout will shift deeper, even though they will continue to cruise the shoreline. Consider a change to a nymph, or even a

*Sandpiper Lake, a turf lake.*

bead-head to fish deeper water. The idea is to cast the fly out across the cruising lane of the trout—you scouted this by watching them from the dawn shadow—and wait for the trout to come to the fly. A dry fly should be floating over the lane or a wet fly sinking down to the trout's level in the lane as the trout approaches.

When a trout approaches, I give a dry fly a twitch, or start to strip a wet fly in slowly. If I get it right, a wet fly will be rising slowly across the trout's line of travel and two feet or so in front of it. I can often watch the trout take the fly, and that makes this a lot of fun. A mistake to avoid is to anticipate the strike when the fish charges the fly and try to set the hook too soon. This will pull the fly away from the trout. Wait until you are sure the trout has taken the fly before setting the hook. See Chapter 6.

After watching the dawn patrol for a while, you may think the trout are cruising a big circuit around the lake. That could literally be true in a small lake. More likely, though, the trout cruise a section of shoreline, and will swim back and forth along it in a circuit that may take as much as ten to fifteen minutes to complete. If you wait you are likely to be able to see the same trout more than once. Many times I have taken a trout on the second or third pass by a rock or log. Getting a "fix" on its route enabled me to get the fly into position in order to make an effective presentation, even if I had to cast well before it came back into view.

Dawn is a relative thing. At a lake in a deep cirque or with high ridges around it, the air takes time to warm and for the sun to hit the water. It might be 9:00 or later, but there is a "sweet spot" of time in the morning when the light and water temperature are right, and the trout patrol inshore. It varies with elevation, weather, time of year, and which part of the lake you are fishing. You may have to start early the first day or two at a particular lake to discover when the dawn patrol starts.

# FISHING SHORELINE STRUCTURE

The trout will have well-established lanes around small peninsulas, rock piles, or logjams that jut off the shoreline. The combination of a small point of land with deep water and structure off the end and shallows on either side is ideal. I fish the near-shore shallows earliest with a dry fly, hoping to hook a good fish or two inches from shore. As the sun rises, changing the amount and angle of light, I anticipate that the trout will begin to cruise deeper and onshore rises will taper off. I then work gradually out to the deeper lanes off the point, switching to a soft-hackle, a standard nymph or a bead-head depending on how deep they are cruising.

If you can spot the trout far enough ahead and can time the cast, the best technique may be to simply let a wet fly drift slowly down into the lane as the trout approaches. That is enough subtle movement to get the trout to strike the fly. More than one observer has noted that trout sometimes ignore a fly the angler manipulates with stripping or twitches, but hit the same fly readily if it is left to drift on its own. Slow-sinking and wind-drifted flies constructed with soft wing and tail materials pulse and flutter creating the illusion of life. I designed the Colonial Coachman fly for the High Sierra with this effect in mind. See Chapter 10.

But if the water is too deep for the fly to sink fast enough or the cruising lane is still in shadow so you can't see trout far enough ahead to time the cast, you may not be able to slow drift to a specific trout. I find the best technique is to switch to a weighted fly and get the fly deeper than the lane, even rest it on the bottom. When a trout approaches, twitch the fly. Stirring up a little mud or debris from the bottom is good if the fly is on the bottom. The action of the fly, seeming to swim up and away from the trout, can prompt a charging strike as the trout attacks this escaping prey.

I call it 'dawn patrol' but shoreline cruising can extend well into the afternoon, especially in the early season. In smaller lakes, the trout may cruise the shoreline more or less continuously. But as the rising sun penetrates the water and eliminates the dawn shadow, the trout are more likely to seek cover in deeper water and cruise the bottom. When you no longer see trout cruising near the shore, it's time to change tactics to cover more water.

*Blazing star.*

## Fishing the Sunny Side

The evening breeze doesn't always concentrate the drift along the shore; the afternoon breeze doesn't always last long enough to concentrate the drift; blow-in may not occur; surface insect activity to create insect drift may not occur. While I start fishing on the assumption the dawn patrol will materialize, and work from the dawn shadow, I also expect to have to fish all around the lake to find the trout if that strategy isn't working.

When trout are located where direct sunlight is already on the water and shoreline, the angler will be far more visible to the trout so that extra care has to be taken to avoid being seen or spooking trout with a cast. Casts may have to be longer and over deeper water, since it's less likely the trout will come very close to the shoreline. At least, they are unlikely to venture anywhere near the spot where you are standing since you will be visible to them. Your clothing and gear will be reflecting several times as much light in the direct sun. (This is why "lime" is out and "mocha" in when choosing a fishing shirt.) Recall that trout can see you as much as sixty feet away. As the sun rises, you lose the advantage within the dawn shadow of viewing structure highlighted by sunlight angled past you into the water. In bright light, surface glare will be a significant disadvantage, and polarized sunglasses are essential to reduce it and give you a chance to see both structure and cruising trout.

The basic tactics of casting over structure and cruising lanes are the same, but the importance of anticipating trout movement is greater. You will have to rely on positioning the fly in or over the cruising lanes you locate or make an educated guess about, to try to intercept the approaching trout. Casting directly over a wary trout in clear, still water doesn't have a high success rate. Line shadow, rod flash, leader wake, and fly splash will all spook the trout. Casting well ahead of an approaching trout or even before a trout is visible avoids alerting the trout with the cast in still water.

Passing clouds that cast shadows on the water present an opportunity to make a cast with a visual advantage. The cloud's shadow masks the disturbance of the line and leader hitting the water, and the passing of the cloud results in a fly suddenly highlighted by sunlight. The results can be dramatic; I've had trout rise at least 10 feet from bottom to take a dry fly-fished this way. Wind gusts which create a passing riffle across the water can be used the same way. Cast across the target structure as the wind-riffle passes, when any line splash will be masked by the wavelets, and wait for the water to settle. After it calms down, give the fly a tiny twitch, and be ready.

As the day progresses and the light increases, I tend to rely on wet flies and nymphs, and occasionally streamers. By fishing subsurface, the leader becomes less visible than it is when outlined overhead in the surface film. My experience is that trout are less wary of taking a fly-fished subsurface in bright light, and it's also less effort for the trout to take it. The tactic of casting across the lane and stripping back across the path of an approaching trout, seen or merely anticipated, is still the basic technique.

This is not meant to imply dry flies won't work when fishing to cruisers in well-lit water. I've had many a day where I kept right on fishing a dry fly from morning to evening. The key was the trout. So long as they were 'happy' with dry flies I was happy to oblige. More typically the response to the dry fly will taper off, and I switch to a soft-hackle or nymph, depending on the depth of the lane I'm fishing and the height of the sun. I return to a dry fly as evening approaches, especially if there are rises visible on the lake.

## WIND DRIFTING

Once a breeze starts up, the wind will create a current in the surface of the water in the direction of the waves. The trout will orient themselves facing into the wind under the choppy surface and cruise searching for insects driven by the wind current. This effect creates a fishing opportunity.

A dry-line cast into the lake cross-wind will soon be pushed along. The fly, which can be wet or dry, will drift in an arc at the end of the leader until the line straightens out along the path of the wind and waves. Since the trout will be oriented facing into the wind and waves, the fly will also be crossing the path of cruising trout as it drifts. This is known as wind drifting a fly.

Observe the lake surface closely during a breeze and an important form of structure will soon be apparent. That is the area of calm water sheltered behind (in the lee of) peninsulas, points of land, coves and islands around the lake. The edge of the wind-current seam where there are waves to one side and smooth water on the other, is usually easy to see. It is also an area where drifting insects are carried and concentrated by the wind and waves. Trout can see the seam or wind line as well as you can and will cruise along it searching out prey. It is excellent strategy to wind-drift a fly along or across the wind seam where you can anticipate there will be trout.

The best position is right at the end of the peninsula or point of land that is providing the shelter from the wind. The current line will extend from there down wind. Cover the water near where you plan to stand with a few short casts first. (You will regret it if a good trout spooks from under your feet as you step up to the shore.) Next cast out to the windward side and let the fly drift with the wind toward and into the seam. If you don't get a rise or strike, then twitch a dry or strip a wet fly a few inches, in or along the seam, and pause. Then twitch or strip again. If still no strike, pick up and cast again, a few feet farther out, and repeat the process, working the fly over the wind seam to the limit of comfortable casting. Since trout may be cruising the seam, it doesn't hurt to repeat the short casts after your longest cast, to be sure you have covered the water along the seam thoroughly.

## WIND DAPPING

Classic dapping is an English and Irish technique for fishing lakes that involves drifting a boat sideways in a strong breeze across a lake, with a long fly rod and floss line that catches the wind. The line is held up in the wind with the long rod so that the fly flips around on the end of the floss line and "daps" or taps the surface of the water. The persistent dapping of the fly gets attention from trout cruising into the wind under waves.

Even without a boat, you can dap using the wind from atop a boulder. It's a technique to know when the wind is too high to backcast well or safely. The trout aren't bothered by wind and you can make it your ally. Although there may be few calm areas that clearly define wind seams on such days, the wind will create lines of foam in the choppy water, which you can see off islands, points and peninsulas, in the same places there would otherwise be a wind seam.

Current slicks may also be evident—these are patches of smooth-appearing water with choppy water around them. The current slicks and foam lines mark concentrations of whatever is borne on the wind and currents, including wind-battered and drowned prey. If you are lucky, the wind will rise suddenly, sloshing and trapping emerging insects struggling to fly. If so, the trout will be hunting them just under the waves.

You will need to find a promontory or boulder that is free of obstacles or trees. Search for one where you can see a foam line or current slick extending downwind from it. Standing directly on top of the boulder or end of the promontory, using a dry line, steeple-cast with the wind at your back. This will cause the wind to catch the line and carry it forward. The fly will tend to splat down, but the water is likely to be so choppy that that won't matter. In fact, it is the first dap.

Lifting the rod tip and the fly line to catch the wind, let the wind flap the line up off the water, and drop the tip so the fly daps again in the area of the current slick or foam line. Repeat to the left, middle and right of the target. Strip line and on the next cast, let the wind 'shoot' the line. Dap again, and repeat, letting out line as you go, covering the foam line. The wind and waves will mask the splashy casting, and you might catch a big trout on the surface in this way.

Wind dapping works well with a two-fly set-up. I use a size 10 or 12 hair-wing fly, such as a Wulff, or a caddis, well dressed with floatant. To the bend of that hook, I tie a ten-inch tippet and add a size 16 soft-hackle or midge pupa. While a two-fly rig is harder to cast, wind dapping doesn't involve a lot of backcasting and the extra fly makes the rig more effective. Trout seem to be attracted to the larger fly, but often end up striking the smaller fly sub-surface. And the force of the wind helps to minimize snarling the leader with the extra fly. In any case, wind dapping will work just fine using a single fly.

Wind dapping sounds more difficult than it really is. It is actually easy to learn if there is enough wind to lift the line and flies. Since you are fishing with the wind, the flies will naturally tend to fall along the foam line. This makes it easy to cover the productive water near the foam line within casting range.

## WHEN THE WIND DIES DOWN

There will be parts of the day and a few entire days when there is no wind and the surface of even a High Sierra lake will become glassy calm. If it is also warm, there may be little or no obvious feeding activity and no rises to be seen anywhere on the lake. The cruising lanes that were productive earlier will seem deserted and there may be no trout in sight along the shoreline. Line splash and the shadow of the line and leader are likely to spook even trout swimming along the bottom.

*Royce Peak from Saddle above Puppet Lake.*

When these conditions are present, there are two basic techniques that will produce trout, even though overall the fishing may be slow. The first is the cast-and-wait tactic, meaning casting a dry fly over likely structure, such as a drop-off, and letting it sit. After a while the ripples and any splash from the cast will die down and the water surface will become still. If the angler is careful not to cause the shadow of the line to move, a trout that eventually comes along cruising the drop-off may take the fly. This can be pretty slow fishing, waiting around for a rise. Just be aware a sudden splashy take may spook you if your attention wanders while you're waiting. I've missed more than a few trout on that account. On the other hand, I've often watched a trout rise several feet through the clear water and take the fly.

The other technique involves stripping a wet fly near structure. The idea is to cast out and let the fly sink. Then slowly and steadily strip line in past or over the structure you are fishing. The angler can be more mobile using this technique, moving along covering the shoreline and casting to structure. Fishing around the lake alternating flies and varying the depth of the

retrieve will help locate the trout and prompt a strike. A long leader is needed so that the fly can sink deep and stay as far from the surface disturbance of the line as possible. I will sometimes switch to a sink-tip line and cast over drop-offs to the shadows of deeper water in these conditions. Even better, I might strip a sunken fly as close to parallel to the drop-off as I can, where it will get maximum exposure to any trout lurking in the gloom of the deeper water. See Chapter 9.

## FISHING FROM SHORELINE BOULDERS

Shoreline boulders that are free of brush and overhanging trees are friends to the High Sierra fly-fisher. There are many obstacles to easy casting around a lodgepole-bound sub-alpine lake, or even a scree-sloped and talus-bound cirque lake above treeline. If there is clear area along the shoreline, even if narrow, steeple and side-to-side casts may make fishing feasible. On the other hand, there are more likely to be thickets of Labrador tea or other shrubs and stunted trees crowding the shoreline that hang up backcasts, grab flies and make casting a hassle. As a sort of Catch 22, the same shrubby shore-line is a rich biotic area that attracts insects and trout.

For this practical reason, boulders rising above the brush and small trees are useful as fishing platforms. While caution is in order when clambering around rocks, the height enhances the ability of the angler to see into the lake with polarized sunglasses and spot underwater structure and trout. Standing a bit higher and away from the brush will allow the angler to backcast further and thus make longer casts and cover more water.

There are two main drawbacks to using boulders as casting platforms. The angler will be much more visible to trout and the height will also cause the line to drop back unless the angler compensates. The drop back occurs when the line, cast from several feet above water, drops the extra distance to the water in front of the boulder. Although the fly will land in the usual manner, there is a longer distance between the rod tip and the water immediately in front of the angler. Instead of a shallow "U" from rod tip to water, there is an "L" formed in the line, from the tip down to the water, and then out to the fly.

As the line falls back it pulls the fly back toward the angler from the point where it landed. This is an unnatural movement. It might prompt a rise from an occasional trout, but is far more likely to generate splash and ripples before the fly comes to rest and spook nearby trout. To compensate, the angler should lower the rod tip to the water as soon as the fly lands. This will avoid disturbing the fly. I will often fish from a boulder with my rod pointed down at the water, rather than raise the tip. This also leaves less slack in the line, so that I can be quicker to set the hook.

Fishing from atop boulders offers advantages that are not obvious. The extra height allows the angler to lift the line off the water, which creates a more direct angle to the fly when setting the hook. The ability to lift more line out of the water also helps in playing a fish. If a larger fish makes a run, the drag of the fly line in the water can break a light tippet. Keeping the rod high when fishing from a boulder and keeping the line out of the water reduces this drag.

Approaching a boulder, especially early in the day when the Dawn Patrol may be in progress, requires caution to avoid spooking any trout near the boulder. If it is feasible, I first cast a fly to each side and off the end of a boulder before climbing up. If the brush is too thick for it to be feasible, then I go cautiously onto the rock, keeping the "low and slow" idea in mind, watching for trout near the base of the boulder. My first cast is usually to the base of the rock. Despite such precautions, many times unseen trout finning in shallows near a boulder have suddenly darted away as I climbed up, leaving me muttering in frustration.

## FISHING FROM SHORELINE LOGS

Along a forested lake shore, there are likely to be logs fallen into the water. There may be several drowned logs or just a single trunk lying against the shore. These fallen logs are allies, since they add nutrients to the water and provide cover for the trout. A fallen log can also be a fishing platform that allows the angler to clear shoreline obstacles to a backcast.

But before stepping onto a log there are a few precautions. Most important is that any bump or thump will be translated into a vibration down the trunk into the water. If trout are using the submerged top of the tree for shelter or feeding nearby, the vibration is likely to scare them away. Before touching the log, cast out from shore if feasible to cover the water along the sides of the log and over the drowned branches. I've often taken several trout before even stepping onto a log.

The second precaution is to test the stability of the log. It may be rotted, or it may tend to rock or roll when you put your weight on it, or sway or bounce as you walk on it. A third precaution is that moss or "slime" growing on it will be slippery. My rule is that if the log has green growing on top, I pass it up. A big splash from falling in is guaranteed to spook just about every trout in the vicinity, not to mention providing endless amusement to anyone who witnesses the event.

If the log checks out, it can then be used as a fishing platform. The biggest advantage of a log, for me, is an obstacle-free backcast, over the water, casting parallel to the shore. This allows me to cover fairly large segments of the shore to left and right, even if there are trees or other obstacles to a backcast along the shore. Getting out over the water also allows me to cover more of the deeper margins of the shallows than I can from the water's edge. See Chapter 9.

## COVERING THE WATER AT TURF LAKES

Turf lakes are lakes above treeline that have a fringe of tundra around the rocky shore. Examples are Emigrant Meadow Lake in Emigrant Wilderness, Merriam Lake above French Canyon, or Wrights Lakes a few miles from Mt.Whitney. There is usually room to backcast around such lakes, but there isn't much structure to give a hint where the trout might be. Typically all you find are a few underwater boulders and a drop-off from the shoreline shallows. The water may drop-off right from the edge three or four feet and shelve out across the lake. The nooks and crannys of the jumble of sub-surface rocks along shore may harbor trout. And trout can be counted on to cruise the edge of the shallow water along the shore, where there will be a transition from light to dark, deeper water. Trout in such lakes ambush prey out from the rocks or in from the deeper water.

Fishing such lakes calls for a modified version of the technique called "fan" casting. Fan casting refers to making casts spaced a few feet apart that radiate around an 180-degrees arc in front of the caster. I have found it is more productive to cast in a pattern that "fills in" the semicircle of lake in front of the angler standing on shore. I call this "grid" casting.

I begin by standing back and casting to the water directly in front of and to the left and right of the spot where I plan to fish. This gives me a chance at any close-by trout I would otherwise spook as I stepped up to shore. I then step to the shoreline and begin to cover the water, casting a few feet deeper, and a few feet further to the left or right in a systematic way, as if filling in a grid. Once I have covered the water in front of me, I then move a few yards along the shore and start again.

This is a disciplined approach. I've found I'm tempted to stay and keep casting over likely structure, on the "There's just got to be one near that rock" hunch. But fishing High Sierra lakes can be counterintuitive since that great-looking structure might be just a bit too deep or too shallow to attract the prey that keep the trout nearby. I catch far more trout moving around the lake and thoroughly covering the shore line than with hunches. If the trout are feeding anywhere near the water's edge, this will eventually present the fly to them.

And that's not to say I don't keep busy catching trout. Many times I've fished a lake shore hooking up a brook or golden trout every two or three casts as I worked around the lake. And every so often, I get an adrenaline-pumping hit from a big trout that takes my line halfway across the lake. The grid approach is not limited to turf lakes. I use it more often fishing them, but I also use it when casting from a boulder or point of land at a sub-alpine lake and I can't tell where the cruising lanes are.

## FISHING INLETS AND OUTLETS

The inlets and outlets of High Sierra lakes can be the best areas to find trout. It depends on the topography of a particular lake. Sometimes the inlet is not much more than water seeping over rocks from uphill snow banks. Other times the inlet or outlet will consist of water running under or draining over large talus blocks. These hardly offer quality habitat. But in other lakes there may be a substantial stream with pools and riffles emptying into or draining the lake. At other lakes, the inlet or outlet may meander through a lakeside meadow. The physical layout dictates how productive the area around the inlet or outlet will be. As a rule, the more flowing water the better, and water flowing through a meadow near the lake will hold at least a few trout.

Water entering or leaving the lake creates inflowing or outflowing currents, and such currents tend to carry prey in their flow. As a result, especially if the bottom is deep or graveled near the flow, trout will cruise the area. It may be a 'way point' in a trout's cruising lane, or sometimes, if the flow is substantial, trout will orient themselves to face into the flow as if it were a stream. Any area where there is inflow or outflow should be treated as structure.

In many High Sierra lakes the inlet area will have a sand or gravel bar, and there will be nothing but shallows with no cover where the inflow actually meets the lake. Fish to the edges and the drop-off of the gravel bar. Even if the flow seems to be a trickle, there may be water flowing through the gravel unseen but felt by the trout, that will keep them in the area. The outlet may also have shallows of built-up sand or gravel. Fishing to the drop-off works there also.

If there is substantial inflow, a current will be created extending out into the lake. This current is actually

*Outlet Creek, path of recruitment.*

flowing over the lake water. Trout will be found under the inflow, and rise up to take prey that is swept into the lake in the current. Sometimes they will be found to the sides of a current, especially if the bottom is shallow. In this hydraulic structure, cast your fly into the current and let it drift out into the lake. If you don't have a hit, then let the fly swing on into calm water and let it sit. Give it a twitch before stripping a wet fly back or picking the line up to cast a dry fly again. This pause gives the trout time to see and react to the fly.

If the inflow is substantially colder than the lake's surface water, the denser cold current will tend to "dive" under the warm surface layer of the lake, creating a sub-surface current. You may have to fish such a current with a weighted nymph or streamer. Because of the consistently low temperatures of High Sierra lakes and typical slow late-season inflows, this phenomenon is not as significant as in lower-elevation lakes with marked thermal stratification. If it occurs, a deep inflowing current can be important structure.

There may be good fishing in the first few pools of the outlet, before it flows away downhill. The same is likely to be true of the inlet stream if it passes through meadows near the lake. Tactics for fishing the stream water are covered in the following chapter.

# Chapter 8

## Pockets Full of Trout: How to Fish a High Sierra Stream

*All this is stream craft, and it is not learned from books; the stream itself and the fish that live in it are the ideal instructors.*

*—Roderick Haig-Brown*

*In little rocky gorges with alternating pools and falls, the creek wandered across a vast meadow . . . In the crystal pockets behind each boulder and at the base of each little fall, the trout were congregated.*

*—Charles McDermand*

ast water is a constant in High Sierra headwater streams. High Sierra creeks and rivers flow over steep gradients and rocky surfaces, only occasionally interrupted by meadows, where the water may slow and meander. Even in a meadow there may be a drop of several feet from end to end. In assessing the fishing potential of a stream, large "car and truck"-size boulders and rocks in a bedrock channel indicate swift and powerful currents at high water during spring snow melt that flush away the smaller stones and gravel. The better habitat will be in the segments of the stream where the rocks and ledges are interspersed with fine gravel and sand, which give a clue that the highwater currents of spring occur with less intensity or duration.

Trout are confined to the flowing water in a stream channel, and the constant pull of the current determines their habits. In cascading mountain streams, currents are strong and they are known to fly-fishers as "pocket water." Trout seek out "pockets" in pocket water, which are the areas in the streambed sheltered from the current as water flows around, over and between objects such as rocks and logs in the streambed. Trout hover in or near the pockets taking prey as it is washed past them in the current.

There is an important reason for this. By holding in a pocket, trout have a better chance of keeping ahead of what I call the Angler's Caloric Law. The Angler's Caloric Law is an unrelenting "law of nature" in streams with fast currents: Trout must take in more calories in the form of prey than they expend holding in the current, or else they starve. If you have ever swum upstream against a current, and felt how quickly the resistance of the water wears you down, you've had a taste of daily existence for a trout in a High Sierra stream.

The Angler's Caloric Law dictates the trout will be found in the pockets of resistance to the current, and that makes presentation very important. To appear natural, a fly needs to drift at the speed of the current to appear to be prey, and it has to drift into the cone of vision of a trout in a pocket, or else it will never be seen coming and won't be intercepted. See Chapter 3. This dictates the basic strategy for High Sierra streams: Fish to the pockets.

*Dawn.*

Even though the current may be unrelenting in a headwater creek, nature provides one precious break in the ruthless pull of gravity on the cascading water. The trout find it in plunge pools.

## ANATOMY OF A PLUNGE POOL

Along the course of even rapidly flowing High Sierra streams are found large and small plunge pools, where the water pours over rocks or bedrock ledges from one level to another. The pool that forms under a waterfall is the classic plunge pool. A stream will actually have a variety of such pools. Below treeline, fallen logs can jam the streambed blocking the water flow. Within the streambed, gravels and rocks can stack up and form small dams which hold back the water. There may be glacier-scoured hollows in the bedrock, filled like so many oversized teacups, brimming with water flowing from one to another. These features have in common water funneled in some manner from one level to the next. The water may be dropping an inch or two, or several feet at a time. But any area where water is pouring from one pool to the next interspersed with flow over bare rock or gravel is good habitat and will hold trout.

The Angler's Caloric Law can account for the "pecking order" of trout in a stream. Trout array themselves in a hierarchy according to size, enforced by the bigger trout which are in the best pockets. When a trout in a good pocket dies—by predation or otherwise—another trout moved up into its pocket. The result is a boost in growth rate for the "new kid on the rock." The boost may be due to more prey passing by the new pocket (more calories), better protection from the current (fewer calories "burned") or a combination of both elements in a prime pocket. A trout that can stay ahead of the Angler's Caloric Law gets social status as well as size.

*Plunge pool.*

*Bubbles and foam are the lid on an important pocket.*

During snow melt in the High Sierra, such a creek will be one continuous, foaming boil of white water end to end. But by mid-June in a year of average snowfall, it will change character. As the melt abates, a pool-to-pool flow will emerge and some of the world's best fly-fishing can be enjoyed. The South Fork San Joaquin River below its source, Martha Lake in the John Muir Wilderness, is a good example. Here the river is creek-size and flows down a turf-matted canyon in a seemingly endless chain of plunge pools, relieved by a few short riffles, for six miles or more before Evolution Creek joins it. This topography and hydrology make the water highly oxygenated. This is a stream that supports hundreds of trout, wild goldens with brilliant orange bellies and carmine-red sides, sparsely freckled with oval black spots, that will pummel any small dry fly.

Plunge pools provide good habitat in such streams because they arrest the power of the falling water, and turn some of it back upstream. As the water pours in like a spout, from inches to several feet high, it scours a hollow in the bottom gravel and rocks. The falling water curls and splits into side currents. This churning water is typically the deepest, most turbulent area in the pool. If not, the deep water will be just downstream of the splash point. When the pool is small, the very head of the pool is where the trout will be, with hiding holes under or near the ledges, logs or rocks over which the water flows.

If the pool is a bit larger, a current "tongue" forms, flowing downstream from the spout. This current will be marked by foam and bubbles formed from the air trapped by the water falling from the spout. The foam and bubbles are a kind of structure and provide cover for trout holding underneath it. It is the "lid" on an important type of pocket.

This pocket is created because the friction of the rock and gravel on the bottom and sides of the pool slows the water flow. The water already in the pool acts as a kind of cushion and the new water splashing in only partially mixes. Most of it flows over the top of the slower water. Trout, obeying the Angler's Caloric Law, will hold in the pocket of slower water under the current tongue (minimizing calories "burned") where they have ready access to any prey drifting in the current overhead (maximizing calories eaten). This pocket is located just downstream from the area of tumbled, turbulent water created by the spout or plunge of water at the head of the pool.

There are two other pockets near the head of a pool, even a small pool. A substantial part of the plunging water spout turned back upstream swirls back against the rocks or gravel under the spout, forming eddies, before circulating back down and eventually out of the pool. Trout will hold in or near these eddies, and in a small pool, the trout holding under the current tongue will foray out from the cover of the foam into the eddies after prey. In a bigger pool there may be trout holding in the eddies full-time.

The energy of the current tongue rapidly dissipates in a larger pool, so that there is an area where the foam and turbulence diminish and the current spreads out and merges into the slow water. This may be a matter of feet or yards downstream, depending on the volume of water, but the best pocket and thus the best trout will be just upstream from the point where the current fades. The reason the best trout are there is that is where the best energy trade-off occurs in the pool. Not only are the trout holding in even slower water than at the head of the pool, but as the current tongue dissipates, any prey carried in the current begins to sink, requiring less effort by the trout to capture.

As the current flows out of a pool, it creates a bar of stones and gravel in the area just upstream of the next ledge or rock dam. The outflow of the pool will accelerate as it flows up over the gravel at the end of the pool, characterized by an area of shallow, smooth, fast-moving water. This area is known as the "tail" of the pool, and the smooth water surface is called the tail "slick." In a small pool, this is another area where trout holding under the current tongue will forage early and then late in the day, when low light provides cover in the shallow water. In a larger pool, this area is likely to have a few small trout holding in pockets, which are often right in front of the rocks or ledge the water spills over into the next pool.

There is another important pocket just upstream from the point where the water shallows out, where the current begins its upward sweep from the deeper water under the current tongue. If there is enough water volume, this spot may be given away by surface turbulence. This is essentially a temporary feeding lie, where trout drop back from slower water upstream early and late in the day. As the water accelerates, the "drag" or friction of the bottom rocks or gravel creates the pocket. Trout hold just above the bottom, and from there will take prey concentrated by the upward flow of the current into the tail of the pool. They typically don't stay in this pocket because it is exposed and is only a partial break from the current. Obeying the Caloric Law, they move back into the slower water after feeding, which conserves the energy taken in.

*Summit sentinel.*

## FINDING POCKETS FULL OF TROUT

The Caloric Law dictates the basic life strategy of all stream trout. They seek out pockets in all sections of a High Sierra stream, including riffles. A riffle is essentially a stretched-out plunge, where the water flows over a slope of bottom rock and gravel before reaching a pool, instead of dropping into it.

The pockets in a riffle are found in the area near rocks where they break up the current. There will be pockets in front, to the sides and behind exposed rocks. Turbulence is created behind sunken rocks in the fast water of a riffle. The pockets will be in front of or to the side of a sunken rock but not immediately behind it.

Pockets are also formed when water meeting a rock in the current splits and flows around it. Water splits, not against the rock, but a few inches or feet (depending on the volume of water and size of the rock) in front of the rock. That space between the split and the rock forms a pocket of slow water called a "cushion." This is often one of the best pockets since a trout has the entire current floating food past it. In other words, bigger trout can often be found "lazing" on the cushions in front of in-stream boulders.

As the water parts and flows around a rock, it accelerates out to the sides and swirls in an eddy behind the rock. This causes the gravel at the base of the rock to wash down past the rock and into the area behind it, making a small sand bar. There are pockets on each side of the rock near the space where the gravel is hollowed out at the base of the rock. Each pocket provides a trout half the current from which to feed. The next best trout are usually found here. Behind the rock, either along the edges of the sand bar or near the end of it, will sometimes be other trout protected by the rock or the sand bar and feeding from the swirl of water flowing behind the rock.

Where several rocks are scattered in the streambed, the currents splitting past the rocks will be merged into what are called "seams" of current. There will be trout to the side of such seams, where current-borne prey is washed along from two or more directions. If fallen logs and other obstacles are in the current, there will be similar pockets in front of or behind them and the trout will seek them out as feeding stations. Because water flows more slowly against and is deflected by irregularities of the banks of a stream, there will almost always be pockets along the rough, bouldered edges of a High Sierra stream or under the rare soil banks where they are undercut.

## FISHING A SMALL PLUNGE POOL

The key to fishing the plunge pools of headwater creeks is simple: Fish small plunge pools as if each was a single pocket. Dry flies or soft hackles are ideal for this type of water. You may not even need to back-cast if the creek is small. Simply flip a dry fly and leader into the pools as you work your way along the creek. Keeping in mind a trout's keen vision, approach each pool "low and slow and from below" or from downstream. See Chapter 3.

In a small pool, the trout will be in the pocket closest to the splash point, and the foam and bubbles will tend to screen the fly from the trout. Instead of casting into the foam, drop the fly first on one side and then the other side of the splash, covering the two eddy pockets. Next drift the fly along the edges of the foam in the current tongue. This will allow the trout holding underneath to see it. It pays to repeat your casts to each area. Such pools can be deceptively deep and it can take two or three tries to get the attention of trout deep under the foam.

You can use a nymph in this type of water but it is difficult to get a proper drift in a short pool, and weighted nymphs tend to hang-up. Instead, flip a nymph down over the little falls so that it sinks under the foam at the very head of the pool. Allow the leader to rest in the current and the fly will swirl and sink into the pocket under the foam. A fish that refused a dry fly may feel more confident under the cover of the foam and turbulence and take the nymph. Choosing a soft-hackle fly for this style of fishing will save having to change flies, since it will still sink if you drop the fly back under the plunge of one pool, but can be worked near the surface as you cover the next pool.

## FISHING BIGGER POOLS

Longer and deeper pools require a different approach. The best trout will be near the point where the foam and bubbles from the head of the pool spread out where the energy of the fast water flowing over the top of the "old" water is finally absorbed. This point may be the deep part of the pool. The bigger the pool the bigger the pocket

*Sierra "steelhead."*

underneath. There may be several trout using it, with the biggest trout just downstream of the point where the pocket begins, and the other trout arrayed in descending order of size downstream of that point.

A dry fly or soft-hackle should be your first choice, since even in a longer pool it may be difficult to drift a nymph down to trout level in a swift current. A steeple or side-to-side cast may be needed if there are rocks or trees behind you. Approach low and slow and from below (slightly downstream) of the last of the foam. There may be one or more trout, and not always small trout, holding in the side pockets among rocks along the bank. To avoid spooking these fish with line or leader or the flash or shadow of your rod, stand back and drift the bank first. When you hook a trout near the bank, land it downstream of the big pocket.

After covering the near bank, cast the fly up into the edge of the foam and let it drift back out of the foam. Next cast a bit further up and over into the current, and drift back over the spot where the foam ends. Keep the fly and leader on your side of the current until you have cast all along the edge of the current tongue nearest you, before you cast past mid-stream to drift the far bank. This helps to avoid "lining" the trout with the line floating overhead.

When you hook a trout, draw it back downstream out of the "sweet spot" to play out and release, to minimize the disturbance to the pool. The thrashing of a hooked trout can thoroughly spook wary trout. It's a good idea as a result to pause and let the pool "rest" and the trout settle down after taking each trout.

*Juniper berries.*

The process of casting to all parts of the pool in sequence from near to far is called "covering the water." Using this technique, catching two or three trout from each pool is common.

## FISHING THE RIVERS

There are substantial streams in the High Sierra, such as the Kern River in Kern Trench, the several forks of the Kings and San Joaquin rivers, or Fish and Evolution creeks. Simply follow a creek down slope and rivulets and small tributaries flowing in will widen the stream and the pools will get bigger. As you study a big High Sierra creek or river you will notice that it is made up of many plunge pools separated by seams of current, staggered across to the far bank, and a few large, slow pools. The hydrology stays the same, and the differences are a matter of scale. Trout will still obey the Angler's Caloric Law and seek out pockets.

The most significant difference to an angler is that there will be a set of pockets, one set for each of the riffles and plunge pools arrayed across the stream. Better still, there will be more and larger in-stream rocks and possibly logs, to create cushions and pockets in the current. Occasionally you will be able to see trout holding in the clear water, but more typically you will have to fish to the pockets.

If you are using a dry fly or soft-hackle, this means "reading the water" (locating the likely pockets), and casting above a pocket to allow the fly to drift down over the target. It is important to know that the surface splash where you see a trout take an insect or strike a fly is not directly over the pocket. Because the trout drifts with the current as it rises, and the ring of the rise also drifts, many anglers are fooled and cast to the point of the rise below the trout's actual position. The pocket will be upstream from where the trout breaks the surface,

### More about the pecking order:

As a hooked trout struggles across a pool, you may observe one or more trout seeming to dash out and follow it. In reality, these fish are defending their pockets. They have no concept of what's happening to the hooked trout, but they know it's swimming across their territory and they challenge it. Trout assert authority by flaring fins (to appear as large as possible) and by "bluff charges" and nips. Often all you see is the flash of the challenging fish while the hooked trout is still deep in the pool, although they might challenge right at the surface. More than once I've said a low, emphatic "Damn" when an impressive fish has sortied out from a covert pocket to set a small cousin straight about boundaries.

After you have drifted the fly on each side and through the current tongue two or more times, try casting to the slow water on each side of or just down from the plunge at the head of the pool. And it may be worth a final cast or two, drifting the fly from the head to the tail of the pool, or as much of it as you can, before moving on. That last drift will often bring up a trout that didn't strike before.

and the fly has to be presented above the pocket to be effective. This is the other reason it is important to learn how to get a drag-free drift—besides appearing real, the fly has to be cast well upstream of the pocket.

In drifting a nymph, timing becomes important. After being cast, a dry fly is traveling on only one plane, on the water's surface. A nymph has to travel in two dimensions, since it needs to sink as well as drift past the trout. Thus you have to allow sufficient distance for a nymph to sink down toward the bottom, as well as drift over the pocket where you hope to take a trout. That requires casting even further upstream. The faster the current the further you will need to cast even if you use a weighted fly.

Working out these variables takes more casting skill than fishing a creek made up of small plunge pools. But the objective is always the same: To drift the fly to that all-important point in front of and slightly above each pocket where a holding trout scans the water. Getting it right is mostly a matter of practice and observation of which casts work and which don't. Even an expert fly-fisher may need to make several casts in the mixed currents of a larger stream to get the drift right to cover a particular pocket with a natural drag-free drift. See Chapter 9. For me, one of the greatest satisfactions in angling is having a big trout take a dry fly in complex currents. Nothing beats a rod bent with a wild rainbow bucking and spraying water out in mid-stream.

## FISHING MEADOW CREEKS

Creeks flowing through meadows pose special problems for the High Sierra fly-fisher. First, the water is typically shallow and the bottom sandy gravel with small pools and undercut banks at the bends and meanders. In places, the creek may split up into more than one shallow channel. This seems like poor habitat, offering little protection or cover from predators, and where the water can warm during midday in summer. On the other hand, a meadow is a fertile and critter-busy place, likely to host numerous insects. As a result, a High Sierra angler may find many wary trout in the meadow segments of a stream.

Trout in a meadow stream have to be approached with care. Low and slow is critical. The best approach is to cast well back from the water, across the grass, allowing only the fly and leader to touch the water. To avoid alerting any trout, you may have to do this from your knees.

The hydraulics of meadow pools is different from plunge pools. The water flow is much gentler in a meadow than in the rocky cascades above it. The meadow is where the gravel, sand and silt from upstream settled. Only where the water flows into a bend will fast spring runoff scour out a hollow two to three feet deep in the sandy gravel and may undercut the bank. Such a pool will be one-sided, meaning the fastest flow will be against the bank, with an eddy on the stream side. The pool will be defined by the bank and shallow gravel above, below and on the outside

edge of the eddy. In summer, the best trout will be holding in the pocket on the bottom under the inflowing current tongue, or next to the bank if it is undercut. There may be one or two smaller trout holding in the eddy along the gravel edge and at the tail of the pool.

Between such pools will be stretches of one- to six-inch-deep riffle water over sandy gravel. Trout may be seen holding right out over the gravel, but this is an exposed lie. Such trout will be extremely wary and require a very careful approach and cast. Any splash or the sight of the leader will surely scare them. On the other hand, such trout may charge five feet or more to grab a dry fly if your presentation is gentle and they haven't seen you.

**An ethical issue:**

In the early season, and as late as August if there is a heavy snow pack, rainbow and golden trout will be spawning in meadow creeks near lakes. If you can approach anywhere close to the trout they are distracted by the biological imperative to reproduce. Spawning trout swim circles and pair up over the gravel. You may see male fish aggressing (snapping and chasing) other trout. Any trout turned on its side flipping its tail is a female digging a nest or covering her eggs. Observe from a discrete distance and move on. Spawning fish sometimes strike at a fly in an aggressive response, but they aren't feeding. Leave them unmolested to make more trout.

Note where meadow trout race off to when you do finally spook them. They will dart for the nearest pool where there is cover. This might be ten yards away or more and completely across the creek. These fish were out foraging in the shallows but their lie is in the pool. Thus, even if a few fish are out over the gravel, fishing to the little pools at the bends of a meadow creek is the key to success.

Fish the pools on the far bank from well downstream, covering the water by casting to the edge of the current tongue where the fly will drift back into the current tongue and along the edge of the bank. A dry fly works best here, since at least 50% of the available insects in a mountain creek are terrestrials.

If there are grassy banks, the pool can be fished from the bank side of the bend. (This is counter to the usual advice about fishing bends in a river.) The deepest water or an undercut bank or both will be just below the grassy edge of the bank. If you drop the fly and leader over the bank at the bend before any trout spot you, the take will be an aggressive strike from the best trout in the pool. This requires a very low-and-slow approach, and you are unlikely to be able to see the fly or the take. Use your ears to listen for the splash and at any twitch or hesitation of the leader, set the hook.

Shallow sand and fine gravel riffles are not the only habitats in a meadow. Meadows can have deep soil and grassy turf. The high, fast currents created during the spring snow melt can cut channels through the grass that are three or four feet deep, but only a foot or two across. Trout use channels as long as the water continues to flow since they have cover and abundant prey. These afford a better chance of success to the angler since the trout's angle of vision is restricted down between the earthen banks. Low-and-slow still applies, and tread softly so you don't announce your presence with thumps and thuds through the soil. Similar tactics apply, drop the fly over the grass bank. If there is brush, you may even be able to get close enough to dap your fly by extending the rod over the channel.

In larger meadows, the creek will tend to wend along and cut a deep bed, exposing gravel and bedrock between soil banks. A good example of this is Cold Creek in Graveyard Meadows along Goodale Pass Trail in the Ansel Adams Wilderness. Such meadow creeks can be hard to fish. The banks only give visual protection to the angler until head and shoulders (or fly rod of the careless)

become visible on the horizon formed by the edge of the bank. At that point any trout below will see you and immediately scatter.

In this type of situation, it's best to fish right from the edge of the water, below the bank, casting upstream. Select a bend, approach low, slow and from below the spot to which you plan to cast. This may be a plunge pool or a riffle pocket in a larger creek. You will have to take the risk of spooking the trout near the point where you step down to the water's edge. From there, cast upstream where the fly will drop ahead of the target and drift into the feeding zone in front of the pocket. Fishing from stream level you will be much less visible. You will be forced to make shorter casts down between the banks, but staying low and below the trout will allow you to catch and release many wild High Sierra trout as you work your way upstream.

What about special situations, the really deep, swift pools you sometimes find in a High Sierra creek, or the mysterious activity at dusk, when you see many rings out in the lake? That's what the next chapter is all about.

*Meadow creek.*

# Advanced Tactics:
## Deep Pools, Dead-Drifting Soft-hackles, a Little Stimulation, Teasing the Margins, Midges and Prospecting for Trophy Trout

*The soft-hackled fly tempts trout a great deal more often. It tempts bigger trout. And it rouses the rapacity of the most lethargic trout causing it to charge from great distance or depth.*

~

*—Sylvester Nemes*

*Vic hooked, played and released a pair of husky one-footers, and spent most of the time atop a huge boulder, casting in all directions. When he hooked and lost a lunker, his remarks of disappointment boomed among the crags for moments afterward.*

~

*—Charles McDermand*

As mentioned in the beginning, there will be days when you can see trout but they just don't seem to cooperate despite what you know is a good cast, or you can't seem to get near the water without scattering fish every-which-way, or conditions make finding trout difficult, such as the "summer slow down" when warm surface temperatures cause the trout to seek the colder, better-oxygenated water in the deeper parts of lakes below timberline. You can still catch trout at such times, but you have to go beyond basics and apply advanced tactics.

The strategies for sight-casting to cruising trout near structure in lakes and fishing the pockets in streams don't change when fishing High Sierra waters. It's the tactics for getting the trout to hit that have to be refined. The refinements are achieving a natural presentation despite physical layout or fast, tricky currents that hinder normal presentation, giving the fly more lifelike movement, stimulating an instinctive strike by the trout, or all three.

## FISHING DEEP POOLS

Many of the larger streams of the High Sierra have very large, deep pools well over six feet in depth. They are characterized by fast inflowing currents over a bottom of large rocks, and are often located in steep-walled bedrock channels that make access difficult. The trout will be found in the usual pockets (see Chapter 8), but the combination of limited access, fast current and water depth will make presentation of the fly difficult. The flycast by a typical angler is whipped across the surface of the pool by drag and he goes away frustrated. But there are ways to fish deep pools in the narrow clefts of High Sierra canyons and come away with a tale to tell around the campfire.

A careful approach is always important. An angler outlined against the bedrock horizon of this pool type will be readily visible to the trout below. This makes it extremely difficult to approach the water from the head of the pool or the sides. Occasionally there will be a ledge screened by brush or rocks to work from, but not often. As a practical matter, a deep bedrock pool will have to be fished from a downstream position. This is a macro application of the "low and slow and from below" rule.

Downstream doesn't necessarily mean the tail of the pool, but means downstream from the trout or pocket you are targeting. And, again as a practical matter, it will often mean fishing from whatever access point the topography allows. This is an area where caution is important. Glaciated, water-polished granite is slick and is often covered with moss or lichen-like plants that are extremely slippery. (The most common mossy plant covers granite with a very thin black coating in the Sierra: black wet rock=danger.) Pass up a spot that you aren't sure you can safely climb down to and climb back up from. Cracking your head and taking a frigid dip into the pool if you slip and fall can be a fatal combination.

I have found two techniques that consistently produce fine trout from such deep pools. These are adaptations of stream tactics developed on less demanding water. The first, for presenting dry flies, is fishing the wiggle or check-cast upstream, and the second, for

*Chain of pools.*

presenting nymphs, is a modification of the Leisenring lift.

The check-cast, which casts a wiggle in the leader, originated as a downstream cast on smooth-flowing spring creeks where even the slightest drag on the fly will put the trout down. But it can be adapted for High Sierra fishing. The check-cast is not really a separate casting method but instead is merely a modified forward cast that throws slack into the tippet.

The check-cast is executed by tipping the rod tip slightly back at the end of the forward stroke. That is what is meant by "check." This has the effect of canceling a minor amount of the energy being passed down the line to the leader and fly on the forward stroke so that, instead of straightening out, the leader will fall to the water in a wiggle or series of small curves. This creates slack in the leader but not the line, if it's done right.

It's all a matter of wrist action. In a normal forward cast, at the end of the power or forward stroke, the thumb of the casting hand ends up pointed at the target when the wrist cocks toward the target. To check the cast and throw wiggle into the leader, tilt the thumb back toward your shoulder near the end of the power stroke. Tilt the rod sharply to create more wiggle, less sharply for less wiggle.

*Nymphing.*

Check-casting a wiggle into the leader allows the angler to create several feet of drag-free drift even in a very fast current. This occurs because it takes a moment or two for the current to pull the fly line and straighten the wiggles in the leader enough to drag the fly. Typically, it is best to cast as directly upstream as you can to the targeted trout or pocket. Ideally, nothing but the fly and leader should land above the trout to avoid lining the trout.

As soon as the fly lands, you will have to start stripping the line back as the current pulls it toward you. This reduces the amount of line on the water, reducing drag, and helps to increase the distance the wiggles float at current speed before straightening out. Stripping takes practice to avoid creating drag yourself by stripping too fast. Do strip fast enough to prevent a bend or "belly" to form in the fly line and drag against fly and leader. Once you get the timing right, the wiggle in the leader will create enough slack to give a drag-free drift over the target trout or pocket. With practice, you can get long smooth drifts that cover several pockets with each cast. Despite the deep, fast water, High Sierra trout will readily rise to any dry fly presented with a drag-free drift.

What may be the most important pockets in a deep bedrock pool are right along the granite banks. Bulges and irregularities in the otherwise sheer surface are enough to create pockets and I have found many nice fish lying right beside the wall. This will be an especially important lie if the current washes against the granite. Where the current tongue passes down the middle of the pool, the best pocket will be just below the point where the current spreads, and in the cushions in front of in-stream boulders. See Chapter 8.

The Leisenring lift is a technique named for Eric Leisenring, an old-time great man of fly-fishing. His claim to fame includes innovations in the design of soft-hackled, fuzzy-bodied nymphs and wet flies. He popularized the lift as a method for fishing mayfly nymphs in the riffles of his native Catskill Mountains in New England. But he also had experience fishing in the West, and may even have been a market fisherman supplying mining camps with fresh wild trout back in the days of 50-fish limits.

At any rate, the lift involves wading out into a riffle and casting a nymph upstream, allowing it to sink, following the fly with the rod tip as it passes by, and then lifting the fly to the surface with the rod tip. This creates a lifelike drift of the nymph along the bottom as the fly passes the wading angler, and then imitates the habits of certain insects, which swim to the surface to emerge. The key was not so much which insect or fly, but that the upward swing of the fly from the bottom triggered an instinctive strike by the Catskill brown trout.

Since trout are trout, the trout in the High Sierra will also readily strike a fly given the same movement. But a pool is not a riffle and a cold, swift High Sierra stream is not a beat on a Catskill mill creek. So the technique has to be modified for the Sierra. First, I don't recommend trying to wade a deep pool, even the tail of the pool. The cold water will quickly create a risk of hypothermia if you try to wet-wade in waist-deep water, among other hazards such as being washed downstream and tumbled over falls if you stumble. Second, the combination of difficult access, fast current and deep water makes it very difficult to sink a nymph very far, much less to the bottom.

But using a modification of the lift, an angler can fish a pool very effectively from streamside. This involves using a type of check-cast called the "pile" cast. The pile-cast means checking the cast hard enough that the fly and leader will spring back in air and fall in a very tight wiggle or pile on the water. When a nymph, especially a weighted nymph, is cast this way, the nymph can sink quickly, pulling the pile of leader under with less resistance. (Drag against the leader tends to pull a nymph up away from the bottom.) Like the wiggle in a check-cast with a dry fly, the slack pile of leader in a pile-cast allows the fly to sink drag-free for a distance, and get down to fish level in the current.

This means casting upstream above the target using a weighted nymph such as a bead head and letting it drift down toward you. How far upstream depends on how much room there is to cast and how fast the water flow is. The faster the flow the more distance is needed to sink the fly down over the bottom rocks where the

*Mountain hemlock.*

*Dead drifting a soft-hackle.*

just before starting the lift. This will help to reduce sideways pull on the nymph against the current.

The trout or pocket you targeted may not be the one that actually results in a take. If you are getting it right, the nymph will sink down just above the rocks and drift for several feet at that level. A trout may take it before you start your lift. Wild trout hit hard, so you'll probably feel the strike. But be alert to any hesitation in the drift and set the hook. A strike indicator will help in fishing a nymph in this manner, but is not essential.

Whether you are fishing a dry or nymph with an upstream cast, you have to be quick to set the hook. The slack you deliberately put in the line with a wiggle or pile cast to get a drag-free drift has to straighten out. That delays the hook-set and allows the trout time to reject the fly, and is another reason to learn and make the "third haul" technique for hook-setting second nature. See Chapter 6.

## DEAD DRIFTING SOFT-HACKLES

The soft-hackle is a type of wet fly tied with a thin body of dubbing or floss and a couple of turns of game-bird hackle, usually partridge or grouse, at the head. See

*Creekside color.*

pockets will be. You will need to start stripping the fly line as soon as the fly hits the water. Strip fast enough to prevent a bend or belly to form that will cause drag, but not so fast as to pull the fly up. If you can strip line back at about the same speed as the current brings it toward you, the fly will continue to sink up to the limit of the length of your leader.

As the tip of the leader approaches, increase your stripping speed until you can lift the line off the water. Ideally the leader knot and an inch or two of leader will hang above the water as the line is passing near you. As it passes, follow the leader knot with the rod tip and at the same time lift the rod tip high, so that the fly will "swim" up from the bottom. This is not the same as letting the current "whip" the fly up off the bottom after the line passes by. An insect rides the current up to the surface. The angler needs to control the action of the fly. In other words, lifting the rod before drag sets in allows the fly to swim up with the current in a more natural way, and that's the action that triggers a strike by nearby trout.

This technique works best directly upstream in a deep, narrow pool, such as below small falls. As mentioned, the best lie may be along the rock edge of the pool, right at the base of a sheer granite wall. But the lift can be used across stream. The difference is the pile will be more quickly straightened out, since the line lying across the current will assert more drag than a line cast directly upstream. And the lift may not be as easy to control, since more line will be on the water. Timing will help here. Begin the fast stripping sooner to reduce the amount of line lying across the current. As the leader drifts down past the angler, it will be further out into the stream. Hold the rod out over the water, swinging it along at current speed so that the tip is as close to vertical over the leader knot as can be managed,

Chapter 10. Possibly because of its simplicity, the soft-hackle is extremely effective. It is traditionally fished "across and down" meaning casting the line toward the opposite bank and slightly downstream. This allows the fly to sink a few inches and "swing" with the current as drag starts to pull against the "belly" in the line. As it does so, the soft-hackle will rise toward the surface. This is thought to imitate the movement of caddis pupae rising to the surface, and I believe it is a movement that stimulates an instinctive strike by trout.

Soft-hackles are even more deadly fished with a dead drift, either across or upstream. If it's dead drifted, meaning at exactly the speed of the current, the soft-hackles of the moving fly will pulse and vibrate in the current, like the legs, "feelers" and antennae of insects, creating the illusion of life. At the end of the drift, as the slightly sunken fly begins to rise up with the pull of the drag on the line, the illusion is complete and that's what prompts rapacious strikes by the trout.

Achieving a dead drift requires learning to "mend" the line. As soon as the fly line lands on the water, the current will exert force against it—the longer the cast the more force. Because the angler is standing still and the line and current are moving past, the line, leader and fly pivot downstream from the rod tip, unlike drifting natural insects which meander with the current downstream. Unless the angler counters it, when the line is cast directly across a fast current the fly will swing in an ever accelerating arc at the end of the leader until it reaches slack water against the bank. Casting upstream and across, and casting a slack line to start with, will help minimize this. Then mending and re-mending the line each time a belly forms will allow the fly to drift at the speed of the current for as long as practicable.

Mending means counteracting drag by flipping the fly line back upstream. That creates an arc in the fly line upstream of the leader and fly and it takes a moment or so for the current to straighten the arc. Repeated mends will allow the line and leader to drift with the current as long as possible without interference from drag. The drift also allows the soft-hackle to sink below the surface, where it is more visible to more trout than a fly on the surface. See Chapter 3.

On many streams the water doesn't flow at the same speed all across the surface. Especially in High Sierra waters, the current will most often be broken into several seams, slots and eddies as it flows over and around instream boulders, logs or other obstructions, each minor current flowing at a different speed. This means mending upstream, if the current between you and the target trout or pocket is flowing faster than the current over the target. Where the current nearest you is slower than the current where the target is, you will have to mend downstream, to avoid having the far end of the fly line, leader and fly pivot from the edge of the slow current, across the faster current, dragging the fly.

Mend so that the line doesn't tug the fly or leader against the current. Several short mends work better in keeping the fly at a constant speed equal to the current, rather than one or two big mends. The longer a dead drift can be maintained the more naturalistic and thus more effective the fly will be. And the suspense won't be long. Trout eagerly take soft-hackles on the drift, even before they begin the swing across the stream at the end of the cast.

But in fishing a soft-hackle, the swing is the culmination. That means adapting the length of the cast and the timing of the drift so that the fly swings across and slightly upstream of the primary target. The swing, especially if the current is fast, may need to be modulated. It's the pull of the current against the fly line as the line finally begins to pivot from the rod tip across the stream, that sweeps the sunken fly up to the surface. Pointing the rod tip toward the fly, and swinging the rod across the stream with the travel of the fly will slow this effect slightly, giving the fly more exposure to the trout. Mending a belly in the line downstream with slack line held in the hand for that purpose, will also slow the upswing of the fly to the surface.

Unless the overall current is brutally fast, the fly can be modulated as it swings through mixed currents as it crosses the stream. This requires a little slack in the line, which is created by dipping the rod tip at the fly, or mending. The idea is to time things so you are giving slack as the fly crosses a slow area, so it will sink a bit, and thus rise again as it hits a faster current. This action undulates the fly up and down, presenting the desirable upswing effect several times as the fly swings across the stream below the angler before it ends the cast, as it finally washes into the bank eddy.

It pays to pause at the point where the fly reaches the bank eddy, and allow the fly to "hang" along the bank for a few seconds. This sometimes prompts a strike from a trout in a pocket along the bank. Stripping the fly back a few yards is also a good practice, to cover the pockets along the bank. In the classic technique, the angler, after executing a dead-drift cast and swing, takes a few steps downstream and repeats the process to cover the water.

## A LITTLE STIMULATION

There are several ways to present the fly as a "teaser," meaning in a way meant to stimulate a strike by the trout. One is "skittering" or skipping a fly across the surface of a stream.

Stoneflies and caddisflies, as well as midges, are insect species that return to the water after metamorphosis into an adult stage to oviposit or lay their eggs. Some simply fly over the water and drop the eggs into the lake or stream. Others dive or crawl back into the water and lay their eggs on bottom structure. But there are several that fly along and land on the water's surface to lay eggs. Certain caddis, in particular, fly over the surface of the water and dap their abdomen, depositing a few eggs each time they pat the water. It is this surface activity of aquatic insects that skittering mimics. And it can be a very effective presentation, especially at dusk when the gloom becomes a form of structure that will embolden the trout and bring them up to the surface.

There is actually a specialized dry fly called a spider, that is meant for skittering. A spider is essentially a

*Shoreline margin.*

fly made entirely of hackle with no body or tail. This forces the fly to ride high up on the hackle tips, where it can be made to skip across the water surface. But any well-hackled fly, such as the Macedonian (see Chapter 10), will work. Since this is a dry-fly technique, a dry line is called for.

Contrary to most of the stream tactics so far described, skittering is best done by casting down stream. This is because, to avoid pulling the fly under, the entire leader has to be kept up off the water. If the leader sinks or drags it will pull the fly under and spoil the cast. Using a short down-and-across cast also helps because drag will tend to pull the line up high in the surface tension, and the line, as well as the leader, needs to ride high on the water to avoid drowning the fly.

The conformation of the currents and any above-water structure dictate the manipulation of the fly. Simply lifting line off the water and pulling back until sufficient line and leader are off the water for the fly to skip back upstream will work, and can be used to skitter the fly "backwards" over the top of likely pockets. But a light touch is needed. Simply generating a vee-wake won't do it. You need to get the fly to hop and dap over the surface, to mimic the naturals.

A skitter is also accomplished by fishing the fly somewhat like the soft-hackle across-the-current swing. There must be a relatively clear water surface to sweep across to avoid hanging up the line on boulders or other obstacles. Because a soft-hackle is supposed to sink and undulate in the current, slowing the swing is good. But

to skitter, the fly will need to move fairly fast to skip over the surface. Keeping the rod tip high, line and leader taut and "checking" the rod will hop the fly over the top of the water.

Skittering really works. It will bring up big trout. And it can often bring up reluctant trout that refused to rise to a standard drift. Even a trout that was spooked, can be covered with a skittered fly and often induced to rise after all.

## TEASING THE MARGINS

There is a time-honored idea in hunting that working the edges of field and forest is the most productive. You jump more pheasants, for example, near the brushy "jungle" in the ditch between the fields than out in the stubble. You find your deer on the edge of the clearing, not out in the open, and so on. This idea is useful in fishing High Sierra lakes as well.

Much of Chapter 7, "How to Fish a High Sierra Lake," dealt with the structure constituting margins in the lake habitat. The drop-off along the transition from shallow to deep water is a margin. The edges of a gravel fan at the inlet form a margin and so on. Trout both patrol and rest along such margins, although they may not be visible. In High Sierra lakes, trout have a special fascination with sunken granite ledges, and take holding positions underneath or patrol along their deepest side. But in such habitats, the structure blocks the view of the trout and you can't often sight the fish.

Trout will play "hide and seek" along such a margin, meaning a trout may engage in a mini-patrol at times, swimming out from behind its cover momentarily before swimming back out of sight. Several trout along a sunken ledge or the base of a cliff-face may engage in this seems-like-it's-completely-random activity. Being alert and ready will give you the chance to cast to a spot where you saw trout, even though the trout may be back out of sight again.

A teasing technique worked along such margins will often prompt a strike. Patience is paramount, since you may have to repeat your tactic many times before you prompt a strike. Using a dry fly, simply make repeated casts along the margin a foot or so apart. If you've spotted a trout, drop the cast nearby and make repeated twitches, 30 seconds or so apart, sufficient to create a "ring" or slight ripple. Casting beyond the edge three feet or so, over the deeper water, is important. The trout can't see through granite any better than you can, so a dry fly has to be placed where it will be within the cone of vision of a trout holding below a ledge edge or lurking in a rock jumble.

Using a wet fly or nymph, a 70-foot cast that strips the fly parallel to the margin, and 10 to 30 inches sub-surface and slightly beyond the break into deeper water is the ideal cast. The irregular nature of most margins and shorelines make this difficult to achieve. As a practical matter, you will be able to obtain only a few feet of the ideal in any given cast. But here again, repetition will pay off. Using shorter casts, cover the margin a segment at a time, until you have pulled the fly past all of the likely water along the ledge or rocks.

A favorite technique of mine is to cast a weighted nymph across a ledge so that it sinks over the edge and down right to the trout. You will have to make an educated guess at the depth over the edge of the ledge, and cast out into the lake far enough for the fly to sink over the structure. After allowing the fly time to sink, strip it back up and over the ledge or rocks. Repeated every three or four feet along the margin, this technique gets the fly right down in front of any trout cruising or holding nearby.

The drawback is that this style can be costly in terms of abraded leader and lost flies. Since you can't

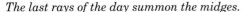
*The last rays of the day summon the midges.*

often see sunken rocks or other obstacles over the edge, hang-ups are a hassle, and as the fly is retrieved, the leader tends to drag across the granite. What helps is to allow the fly to sink slowly, but strip it back quickly so it (hopefully) will skip over anything it bumps, including the ledge. I have taken more than a few nice trout that eagerly took a nymph fished this way, since I was well out of view above the ledge.

A standard forward cast works well for these teasers, but learning the roll cast will make repetitive casting easier. The roll cast is not difficult and may be one of the easiest casts to learn. A roll cast is essentially merely throwing a loop into the line without lifting it off the water. Watching a video or having someone show it to you is better than trying to use words to teach it. But it is done by lifting the rod and drawing the line back toward you, holding the rod high, until the line hangs from the tip just past your ear (right ear if you cast with your right hand) and a couple of inches to the side of the reel. Pause, and then execute a forward or power casting stroke to start the cast. The combination of the inertia of a dry line held in the surface tension of the water and the energy of the casting stroke, which breaks the water's grip, will cause the line to lift off the water in a progressive loop that rolls out in the direction of the cast, and turns the fly over and onto the target. With practice you can even shoot line with a roll cast. Since there is no backcast, it is especially useful along a brushy shore.

I use the roll cast so often I carry a double-taper line into the High Sierra. Roll casting is much easier with a double-taper line (which rolls heavier line over the lighter tip) than a weight-forward line (which rolls lighter running line over the heavier tip), but with practice it can be done pretty well even with a weight-forward line. And it can be done with a sink-tip line or even a sinking line, although that's more a challenge than a needed skill. With a sink-tip the key to roll casting is not to try to cast too much line and to draw the line back quickly so that as much as possible of the sink-tip is pulled up to or near the surface, and immediately execute a hard stroke using the rod's reserve power to roll over the sink-tip while it's at the surface.

Use the same technique fishing a weighted nymph on a dry line. Use the rod tip to lift the nymph as you draw the line back toward you to get your fly up near the surface before casting. Done right, the nymph will pop right out of the water when the line rolls past and plop back down near the target. Roll casting a nymph every three feet or so along a margin is very effective, even on days when there are no cruisers in sight and no other visible feeding activity.

## MIDGES

Midges are true flies, Diptera, and as mentioned in Chapter 2, are an important part of the diet of High Sierra trout. There are many lakes where midges and blow-in (see Chapter 7) are the principal forage base of the trout. As a general matter, midge larvae are burrowing insects, which inhabit bottom mud and debris. They are not often available to trout until they pupate and swim to the surface to emerge. Pupae hang under the surface film before emerging. In the Sierra, midges range in size from the famous size 14 blood midges of the Truckee River drainage, down to tiny winter emerging blacks size 24 and smaller.

For the trout, midges are a good news/bad news proposition. Once a hatch starts, midges can emerge by the millions per hectare of surface area of a lake. Yet they are so small trout have to consume them by the hundreds. Midges require fairly quiet water to hatch, so that there are few if any midges in cascading High Sierra creeks and rivers.

Where they are found, midges can emerge just about any time of day, just about any time of year. But the arch-typical hatch is at dusk in mid-summer, after the wind dies down, when the glassy smooth surface of a lake suddenly becomes alive with the "dimples" of rises and the bulges and swirls of trout feeding just under the surface. These trout are foraging on the pupae as they near the surface after rising up from bottom, or the pupae hanging under the surface film waiting to break through, and less often on the hatched adults on the water's surface or hovering just above it.

A two- or three-fly rig has worked best for me. I set-up the rig using a dry fly, with a midge pupae trailer tied to the hook gap of the dry, and if I use one, a second trailer tied to the first. I also sometimes rig using dropper loops (see Chapter 11), with the dry at the end of the leader. 6x tippet will work well for size 18 to 20 flies. The dry fly is basically a strike indicator. Although I've often had hits on the dry, the trout are more likely to strike the trailing fly.

There are two keys to success when fishing a midge hatch. First is to follow your fly so you know where you've cast and can see a strike. Second is to bear in mind the small cone of vision or window of a trout at the surface. See Chapter 3. At the surface, a trout's window is only a foot or so across. The naturals are so numerous, the trout can wander in a haphazard way right under the surface gulping them down despite the small window. This makes effective presentation difficult, because the fly has to be cast very near the trout and it's difficult to anticipate rises.

To solve the problem of knowing where your flies are in dim light at dusk, I evolved the "Visible Griff" from the Griffith's Gnat, specifically for this purpose. See Chapter 10. But any dark fly tied parachute style with a white post wing in the size 16 to 20 range can be substituted. The white wing makes it much easier to see where your flies are.

The solution of the problem of where to cast begins with the idea you have to intercept a trout with the cast. One approach is simply to cast in the general direction of the rises. This essentially relies on luck to guide a trout past your flies. If you are making very long casts when visibility is marginal, then this may be the only practical presentation. To hedge your luck, a slight twitch of the dry when a rise is spotted nearby is called for. Slight is the key here; too-aggressive twitching may put the trout down.

*Study structure from a vantage point.*

A second method is to try to single out a trout from the pattern of its rises and deduce its general direction of travel. Targeting that specific trout, your cast should straddle its anticipated route with the flies falling a few feet from the last rise. Be prepared to be patient; trout feeding in this manner have a disconcerting habit of rising in a spot having no obvious connection to any previous rise and far from your cast. If you can still follow the trout, you will have to pick up and cast across its anticipated route once again.

As a third approach, using a dry only, I have sometimes had luck putting the fly right in the ring of the rise at dusk. This takes a careful cast, so that the fly lands gently. It also takes quick reflexes, since the fly has to get there right away. A delay of more than a few seconds will mean the fly will be well out of the trout's small window, as it swims on.

A trout's take of a midge fly is usually very subtle and difficult to detect subsurface. This is where the dry functions as a strike indicator. Any movement of the dry on a calm surface should be interpreted as a strike, and the rod tip should be raised to set the hook. Using small midge flies, a trout is often unaware of being hooked until resistance is felt. Thus there can be a delay before the trout reacts. If you are using a very light tippet, you will need to keep slack line in your stripping hand and immediately feed it out when the trout turns and starts to run to avoid a break-off.

## PROSPECTING FOR LARGER TROUT

Sooner or later, as noted by Hewitt in the quote in the introduction, every angler has a hankering for catching larger trout. There is a bit of the brag in taking bigger fish, but also an element of challenge and satisfaction that your skill level has gone beyond ordinary. In the High Sierra, with its short season of growth and limited biomass, finding larger trout becomes a challenge in itself. There are plenty of good trout in the Sierra, as discussed in Chapter 3, but they are not present everywhere. You will have to prospect for them.

The traditional advice is you have to go where other anglers seldom go and the water isn't "fished out." That wisdom is based on an assumption that if the fish weren't being caught and kept, they would always grow large. Even if sometimes true, this notion breaks down in the High Sierra because just being left alone doesn't ensure the trout will grow to size. The quality of the spawning habitat and productivity of the lake or stream are far more important than angling pressure. To be sure, catch-and-keep angling will soon reduce the number of larger trout no matter where the water is.

But in the Sierra, abundant clean, cold water and good spawning habitat tends to result in high survival rates and thus heavy competition for the available food. A balance is eventually reached, between the trout and the prey, where the maximum number of trout consistent with prey survival is sustained. Many times this means there will be an abundance of 6- to 8-inch golden or brook trout, but few 14-inch fish, as mentioned in Chapter 3.

Prospecting for larger trout requires finding lakes where the number of trout are low but the basic productivity is good. This is usually determined by an absence of spawning habitat or poor spawning habitat and big water. This is not always the case, as there are numerous small lakes in the subalpine belt that are very productive. But above treeline, I have found larger trout more consistently in lakes having surface area 15 acres or more. Sometimes these are shallow lakes with a lot of surface area, and sometimes are lakes subjected to

periodic winter-kill that are replenished from nearby streams or other lakes.

The other factor is the Department of Fish and Game planting schedule. Lakes with no or only limited spawning areas have trout because they are planted, and other waters receive "supplemental" plants from time to time. It's pretty easy to tell a lake has been planted within the last two years because, "mysteriously," almost all the trout you catch will be identical in size. After two years the survival rate starts to fall off, so that the remaining trout will begin to show differing growth rates and, unless a new plant occurs and reduces the food base, a few may make it into the 15-inch class. One place worth prospecting, then, is a lake in the third or later year after planting.

Within a lake basin, the quality of available spawning habitat and productivity of each lake can vary widely, so that some lakes will offer consistently great fishing and others will grudgingly yield only a few trout. There may be small "lakelets" between larger lakes, along the connecting streams, that contain trout. The concept of "recruitment" is important here. Recruitment refers to the upstream or downstream migration of trout from a lake or other resource. Both golden and brook trout readily colonize the inlet and outlet creeks of the lakes where they are introduced and soon spread into nearby tributaries.

Recruitment is not always voluntary. In spring, after snow melt, lake levels may be high and the outflow

*Wild golden.*

swift. Lakes in hanging canyons often have falls below the outlet. Young-of-the-year trout are not strong swimmers and if caught in the current will be swept down the outlet stream. This can be fatal, but also can result in downstream recruitment of the survivors into a lake or lakelet that otherwise would not have trout. If that lake also has poor spawning and at least fair productivity, the relatively small number of trout recruited into the lake will have a chance to become trophies.

Remoteness is also a factor. Seldom-visited lakes are unlikely to receive routine plants, and many once planted lakes are not replanted (or "orphaned"), resulting in the potential for a few larger trout to survive. Orphan lakes aren't the only redoubt of big trout. The basic quality of the water is most important. I can think of several lakes near Mammoth Crest, that despite their reputation and popularity, and thus fishing pressure, produce a few really nice trout year after year.

Lake basins, chain lake canyons or areas where there are clusters of lakes, offer the best chances of finding larger trout. You can begin prospecting by studying maps to find such areas and plan a trip to visit as many lakes as you can. Doing a little homework and checking into planting records by calling the California Department of Fish and Game office or a state hatchery near where you want to go, will help to narrow down the choices. Contacting the fishery biologist (who may be a state or federal employee) responsible for the area to ask about its prospects, can give you a better idea of what to expect and maybe a hint about which lakes to try.

But there is no substitute for scouting the water directly once you get there. To fish a lake basin or chain of lakes, I day-hike from a base camp. Each day I head out to prospect one or more lakes, until I have visited each lake to see what it has to offer. If I find something interesting, or an area I especially like, I may move camp to that location. But more typically, I will work from the base camp and simply return to water I find productive.

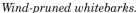

*Wind-pruned whitebarks.*

*Wrights basin.*

I try to cover all the lakes and streams, since it's easy to miss something. I may re-visit a lake, especially to fish it at a different time of day, if the lake showed potential on the first visit. Assessing a lake's potential means finding a vantage point from which to study the shoreline structure, and then to watch for cruisers. You may need to climb a ridge or plan a route that will provide an overview. From above, ledges, shallows, channels, and similar structure will be far more evident than from lake level.

Even if you've found interesting structure, to get a true sense for a lake's potential you will need to catch several trout. If you quickly catch five or six 6-inch trout, and haven't seen any larger trout cruising, that tells you something about what the lake contains. While it's a good idea to fish for a while, to make sure you didn't miss something, if the objective is a big trout it's probably time to move on. I prefer to explore the entire shoreline of each lake, but that may be impractical at a big lake or chain lake series due to time or topography. Minding what I saw from my vantage, more often I concentrate my fishing at the most promising areas of each lake. See Chapter 7.

The biggest disadvantage of the base camp approach is that it seldom puts me on the outlying lakes at dawn or dusk during the late summer. It takes time to hike to outlying lakes and to hike back to camp before dark. For this reason, I try to assess which will be the best lakes in selecting a base camp, and choose a site that will have reasonably quick access to them. This is typically along a creek, or on an isthmus, between lakes. This allows me to cruise the shoreline of the nearest lakes on my way out or later on the way back, and thus cover the prime water during prime time.

But what about flies? Aren't they the direct interface with the wild in all this? The next chapter covers both old and new flies that consistently take High Sierra trout.

# Chapter 10

# Angler's Edge:
# Flies and Fly Patterns
# for the High Sierra

*They fasten red wool around a hook and fix onto the
wool two feathers which grow under a cock's wattles
and which in color are like wax.*

*–Aelian, c. 200 B.C.*

*They sit high and delicately on the water, are usually
floated over the fish without artificial movement and
their patterns are impressionistic rather than attempts
to imitate some specific insect.*

*–Roderick Haig-Brown*

any standard patterns are productive in the High Sierra. As explained in Chapter 2, the trout are opportunistic foragers and have only incidental periods of selective feeding. The best flies are suggestive of a class of insects rather than matching any single species. The Elk Hair Caddis, for example, resembles several different caddis species without being exact to any. The only match-the-hatch fly I routinely use matches a terrestrial, the black carpenter ant.

I am an unabashed fan of the soft-hackle fly: Simple to tie, suggestive rather than exact, easy to fish, and very effective at catching trout. Flies styled to give the impression of life by subtle flutter and movement of soft, translucent materials without attempting anatomic precision is the ideography of a new school of tying. Even the simple innovation of adding a soft-hackle to nymphs such as the Hare's Ear or Zug Bug is part of the "movement."

A dedicated fly-fisherman, Sylvester Nemes, almost single-handedly brought the English style of soft-hackle flies back from obscurity in the mists of the English border rivers, to their current popularity in western North America with his book *The Soft Hackled Fly*. His book was part of the trend toward creating flies that are impressionistic rather than realistic. James Leisenring, an angler mentioned earlier in this book, called it creating an "effect" in his book *The Art of Tying*

*the Wet Fly*, first published in 1941. I followed their trail in designing the Colonial Coachman specifically for the High Sierra.

I update older patterns, such as the Captain, Grey Hackle Yellow, and California Coachman, with modern materials to make them more durable for use in the High Sierra. The Visible Griff' is simply a small step toward making an excellent fly even better. The Grey Soft Hackle and Minimalist Damsel are simple flies that have proven themselves over and over in all types of water, as has the Lime Soft-hackle. The Mountain Midge is a "quick and dirty" pattern that is easy to tie on a small hook and that motivates trout. The Neme-sys is a tribute to a great angler.

Streamers and nymphs larger than size 10 are not recommended in the High Sierra. Size 6 and 8 hooks (common sizes for Woolly Buggers and similar flies) are big enough to stab a small trout through the eye, brain, heart or gills. You will hook and release many small trout so that flies tied on barbless or crimped barb size 10 or smaller hooks are more suited to the High Sierra. A large fly can be tied by using a long-shank hook of size 10 or 12 to build up an oversize body over the smaller hook gap, if you believe size is essential. A list of patterns commonly stocked by fly shops and other sources and the sizes that I do recommend are included at the end of this chapter.

## DRY FLIES

### Macedonian

Aelian, the ancient Roman writer quoted on the facing page, was describing a fly used in Ancient Greece. His famous comments are one of the earliest references to fly tying known. In the translation at least, the trout "maddened by the color comes straight at" the fly. That's a heck of an attractor pattern. Aelian didn't say more about how the fly was tied but, given the freedom for "interpretation" inherent in archaeology, here's my inspiration:

| | |
|---|---|
| **Hook:** | Mustad 94833, size 10-14, or equivalent |
| **Thread:** | Red |
| **Tail:** | None |
| **Body:** | Red wool |
| **Hackle:** | One brown palmered, one brown wound at eye |
| **Wing:** | None |

**Tying Note:** Naturally cock hackle is called for. Use a single strand from wool yarn. Heavily hackled flies tend to spin when cast. To counteract this, the palmered hackle should be wound concave side to the rear, and the eye hackle wound concave side forward, or the reverse. This splays the barbules around the hook with opposite bias and cancels out the spin otherwise created.

### Captain

The Captain was a fly Charles McDermand mentioned many times in his books about fishing the High Sierra, *Yosemite and Kings Canyon Trout* and *Waters of the Golden Trout Country*. Lake McDermand is named after him. But McDermand didn't describe many of his flies, I guess in the 1940s everyone knew which flies he was talking about. This was all he said about the Captain: "This fly looks like a Royal Coachman except that it's thin, shiny black body is tied of black silk." I couldn't tell for sure from this how the fly was dressed and was getting discouraged after trying to find the 'recipe.' Then one day at Mel Cotton's Sporting Goods in San Jose, California, before they remodeled, I was searching around in an old fly case and there in the back of a drawer were six size 12 Captains. I have no idea how long ago they were tied, nor the fate of the other odds and ends in that case. But I was very eager to try them and bought all six. Two I put away in my "archive." The rest? Yep, they're deadly.

| | |
|---|---|
| **Hook:** | Size 12-14 Mustad 94845, or equivalent |
| **Thread:** | Black |
| **Tail:** | Pheasant tippet |
| **Tag:** | Gold tinsel |
| **Body:** | Black silk or floss |
| **Wing:** | Quill |
| **Hackle:** | Brown |

## Captain

Here's my updated version:

| | |
|---|---|
| *Hook:* | Size 12-16 Mustad 94845, or equivalent |
| *Thread:* | Black |
| *Tail:* | Golden pheasant tippet |
| *Tag:* | Gold tinsel |
| *Body:* | Black polypro yarn |
| *Wing:* | Calf body upright & divided or calf tail Trude style |
| *Hackle:* | Brown |

**Tying Note:** Quill wings don't hold their shape even when reinforced with glue. Hair is far more durable and floats better. Jack Dennis, in the first edition of *Western Fly Tying Manual,* lists another version of this fly with an ostrich herl body. But silk, floss, and herl are absorbent. Polypro is colorfast and won't absorb water. As sold, polypro yarn is too bulky for small flies right off the card; instead split off a few strands and wrap a tapered body.

## Dun Hackle Yellow

| | |
|---|---|
| *Hook:* | Size 16-18 Mustad 94845, or equivalent |
| *Thread:* | Yellow |
| *Tail:* | Dun hackle fibers |
| *Body:* | 3/4 "dirty" yellow, 1/4 pale olive dubbing blended |
| *Rib:* | Fine gold tinsel or wire (optional) |
| *Hackle:* | 3 medium dun |

**Tying Note:** The dubbing should be spun tightly and the body tapered. You can substitute pale-yellow polypro for the body. The fly is essentially similar to a Catskill "variant" except the tail and hackle should be tied full because this is a Western fly intended for pocket water.

## Grey Hackle Yellow

The Gray Hackle Yellow is a very old pattern from the "dawn" of fly-fishing, and was another fly mentioned over and over by McDermand "catching" at various lakes and streams of the High Sierra. It's still a popular fly and remains effective presented as a wet fly after it has been dunked a few times playing fish.

| | |
|---|---|
| *Hook:* | Size 12-18 Mustad 94845, or equivalent |
| *Thread:* | Black or yellow |
| *Tail:* | Red hackle |
| *Body:* | Yellow floss or dubbing |
| *Rib:* | Gold tinsel (wire on 18) |
| *Hackle:* | Grizzly |

**Tying note:** "Gray" was an old English term for grizzly hackle. A version of this fly has a peacock herl body and is known as Gray Hackle Peacock. You get the idea for this old-style pattern. Hackle that is actually gray in color is known as "dun" hackle. Simple isn't it? Anyway, one of the most common and widespread mayflies in Sierra Nevada streams is the pale morning dun (PMD for short). The natural is a shade of dark or "dirty" yellow, sometimes with an olive tinge. A more modern high-floating version we'll call Dun Hackle Yellow follows.

## California Coachman

This is one of my 'nostalgic' favorites. I read once that it may represent a phase of the green drake mayfly's life cycle. I don't know about that; to me it is more suggestive of the adult yellow stone (*Isoperla*) of Sierra streams. In any case, it is a great fly and I've caught an awful lot of High Sierra trout with this pattern.

| | |
|---|---|
| *Hook:* | Size 12-14 1x long |
| *Thread:* | Black or yellow |
| *Tail:* | White (Amherst) pheasant tippet |
| *Butt:* | Peacock herl |
| *Body:* | Yellow floss |
| *Thorax:* | Peacock herl |
| *Wing:* | White quill |
| *Hackle:* | Yellow |

## California Coachman

I've updated this fly as well, to make it more durable. Here's the recipe:

| | |
|---|---|
| **Hook:** | Size 12-14 1x long |
| **Thread:** | Black or yellow |
| **Tail:** | White (Amherst) pheasant tippet |
| **Butt:** | Peacock herl |
| **Body:** | Yellow floss |
| **Thorax:** | Peacock herl |
| **Wing:** | White calf body (upright & divided) or calf tail (Trude) |
| **Hackle:** | Yellow |

**Tying Note:** The wing tied "Trude" style gives it a caddis profile. You will have to ask the trout what they think it is. Herl and paste floatants don't mix—they tend to mat the herl and it loses its luster. Better to dab a little paste floatant on the tail and wing of this dry fly. Use the larger herl from peacock tail feather for a dry fly, not "strung herl" which is body feather better used for wet flies.

## Visible Griff'

George Griffith's Griffith's Gnat is a reliable midge fly. It is supposed to imitate either an adult midge or cluster of midges. It is typically productive when cast to trout rising to midges. However, it is difficult to see at dusk or on overcast days. The following pattern will help cure that problem. The name is a play on another old pattern known as the Bivisible which also uses contrasting hackle colors.

| | |
|---|---|
| **Hook:** | Size 18-22 Mustad 94840, or equivalent |
| **Thread:** | Black |
| **Body:** | Peacock herl |
| **Hackle:** | Grizzly palmered over body and a few turns of white or pale cream cock hackle at eye |

**Tying Note:** The softer hackle from a saddle should be used to palmer this pattern, but stiff white or cream dry-fly hackle from a cape is best, wound just back of the eye. To keep the fly floating low in the surface film, clip the light hackle from under the eye of the hook, leaving a fan of white indicator hackle above water.

## Foam Black Ant

This is another very simple fly. It uses modern prefab materials in the form of high-floating precut closed-cell foam. It imitates the carpenter ant which is a common insect in and around lakes and streams of the High Sierra at or below timberline as its name implies. Trout love ants, and they are common fall-in or blow-in insects. I used this fly to catch the brown trout on the back cover of this book. I spotted it cruising in a lake in the Yosemite National Park back country. I cast the fly from across a small cove (where I was out of sight) and under an overhanging pine bough so the fly would appear to have fallen from the tree. It is a very durable fly that will take some abuse. The naturals crawl over the dry rocks along a creek bank and fall or are brushed by wind into the water. Bouncing this pattern off the boulders into pockets produces great fun.

| | |
|---|---|
| **Hook:** | Size 12-14 Mustad 7957B, or equivalent |
| **Thread:** | Black |
| **Body:** | Precut black foam |
| **Wing:** | Honey dun hackle tips (optional) (Photo) |
| **Hackle:** | Black |

**Tying Note:** This is an easy fly to tie. Lay a thread base, wrap back to the 2/3 point, crimp the foam with 3 or 4 loose wraps and bind down with 6 to 10 more, making a base for the hackle. Tie-in the wings with tips pointing back "Delta" style before the hackle if you opt for them. I use good black cape hackle but one size small and make only three wraps of hackle to suggest legs, which can be clipped underneath to be more realistic. Tie off and cement. Although 7957B is a wet-fly hook, the shaft length of a size 10 7957B hook is almost exactly the same length as a Sierra worker carpenter ant. The heavier hook keeps the buoyant foam lower in the water, and the hook will hold up to rough use and repeated sharpening much better than light wire.

# KILLER SOFT-HACKLES

## Colonial Coachman

I designed this fly specifically for fishing the High Sierra. In fishing parlance it could be classified as a "searching" fly, roughly based on the old English patterns known as Partridge & Herl and Leadwing Coachman. It's meant to be stripped over shallows and drop-offs of lakes, or dead-drifted on a stream. It lacks a 'redcoat,' but I added a 'periwig.' It has elements intended to suggest mayfly emergers, caddis pupae, as well as damselfly or dragonfly nymphs and has proven very effective.

| | |
|---|---|
| **Hook:** | Size 10-16 Mustad 3906B, or 1x long equivalent |
| **Thread:** | Black or olive |
| **Tail:** | Brown marabou |
| **Rib:** | Copper wire |
| **Body:** | Peacock herl |
| **Wingcase:** | 'Ball' of gray dubbing |
| **Hackle:** | Brown partridge |
| **Bead head:** | (optional) |

**Tying Note:** Don't overdo the tail. The copper wire can either be counter-wound over the herl or the herl twisted around the wire and wrapped. To add a little weight, wrap a wire base for the dubbing, after ribbing the herl. The gray dubbing should be compact to suggest the "ball" of an emerger's wings. It will also flare the hackle. Take the partridge from mid-back, which has brownish-gray barbules, not the covert feather from the wings with the tan stripe down the middle. Tie with a bead head to add more weight. I substitute a longer yellow & brown mixed marabou tail on a bead head, to jazz up the color scheme and emphasize the up-and-down "jigging" motion of a stripped bead head.

## Grey Soft-hackle

This is a simple fly but it is a mainstay of mine. It is an all-purpose lake fly. It can resemble rising caddis pupae, *Callibaetis* emergers, and who knows what else, thanks to its simplicity. I also use it in streams, in the usual across-and-down method for soft-hackles, or with the Leisenring lift technique (See Chapter 9).

| | |
|---|---|
| **Hook:** | Size 10-14 Mustad 3906B, or 1xl equivalent |
| **Thread:** | Black |
| **Underbody:** | 6-8 wraps medium lead wire |
| **Body:** | 'Adams grey' dubbing or wool |
| **Hackle:** | Brown partridge, grouse, or mottled hen back |

**Tying Note:** The dubbing should be tightly twisted and the body tapered over the lead underbody. The hackle should be tied just forward of the lead, to flair it slightly. This will give the hackle fibers more movement as the fly is down-drifted or stripped.

## Lime Soft-hackle

This is a fly I worked up for fishing small High Sierra creeks. It's a bit unorthodox in the tying method, but the end result is very good indeed. It has accounted for countless golden and brook trout.

| | |
|---|---|
| **Hook:** | Size 14-16 Mustad 3906, or equivalent |
| **Thread:** | Black |
| **Body:** | "Lime" fluorescent floss (Depth-Ray or equivalent) |
| **Abdomen:** | Sparse hare's ear |
| **Hackle:** | Gray partridge |

**Tying Note:** The unorthodoxy is that the floss is cemented to the hook, rather than wrapped over a thread base, and is tied in with only two layers. Wrap a thread base only 1/3 of the way back from the eye, and tie in a single strand of floss. (You will need to separate four-strand floss.) Coat the hook with head cement and wrap the strand back to the bend and back forward to the tie-in point, and secure it. The wet cement will make the floss transparent; the color will return as it begins to dry. After it's dried, dub a sparse bit of hare's ear on the thread and make two or three tight wraps to form a thorax. Tie in a prepared gray partridge breast feather, wrap forward, and tie off. Although cementing the floss is new, the idea of a very slender colored abdomen is an old idea in the design of soft-hackles, going back to the nineteenth century at least, when silk was used. In my fly, the bright combination of the hi-vis floss and speckled hackle will bring hard strikes all day long. Tied on a size 6 hook, it makes a fine summer steelhead fly to boot.

## Partridge, Tan & Brown

This pattern is intended to represent the *Callibaetis* mayfly. Dense populations of mayflies are rare in the High Sierra, but this may be the most widespread and common mayfly in Sierra lakes and the one most likely to be encountered. The *Callibaetis* is a plant-loving swimming nymph, so that stripping the fly over or near aquatic vegetation is a good strategy.

| | |
|---|---|
| **Hook:** | Size 12-16 Mustad 3906B, or equivalent |
| **Thread:** | Tan |
| **Tail:** | Partridge |
| **Underbody:** | Ribbing (optional) |
| **Body:** | Rear 2/3 tan, front 1/3 dark brown dubbing |
| **Rib:** | Fine gold or copper wire |
| **Hackle:** | Brown partridge |

**Tying Note:** This is basically a soft-hackle, so the abdomen should be slender. Dub the rear 2/3 of the hook shank with the tan material, and rib forward. To add weight, use ribbing to wrap a wire base for the thorax. Since mayflies are found in shallower parts of a lake, heavy weight is not called for. Dub the last 1/3 with dark brown material to represent the thorax, and wrap the soft hackle. *Callibaetis* sometimes have an olive tint so a little pale olive blended into the tan dubbing will give this pattern universal fish appeal.

## Neme-sys

Sylvester Nemes' book *The Soft Hackled Fly* taught me a lot. I named this fly in his honor, even though it is not quite true to the old English style.

| | |
|---|---|
| **Hook:** | Size 12-14 Mustad 3906, or equivalent |
| **Thread:** | Olive |
| **Tail:** | None |
| **Rib:** | Gold wire |
| **Body:** | Rear 2/3 olive-dyed pheasant tail, 1/3 ruddy pheasant tail |
| **Wing:** | None |
| **Hackle:** | Gray partridge |

**Tying Note:** Wind an olive abdomen counter-wound with wire and thicker ruddy thorax to suggest a mayfly nymph. This fly is intended to bridge between a standard nymph and traditional soft-hackle, such as the original Partridge & Pheasant. But in that it may be imitative of a broader range of insects than the rising caddis pupae traditional soft-hackles are thought to represent. That is, a trout's nemesis, like Mr. Nemes.

## TWO MORE THAT WILL ADD TO YOUR SCORE

### Minimalist Damsel

The damsel nymph is a relatively large and active insect that swims around plants and other structure in shallow areas, hunting for anything smaller than itself to feed on. The following pattern is a stripping fly, durable and easy to tie:

| | |
|---|---|
| **Hook:** | Size 10-12 Mustad 9672, or 3xl equivalent |
| **Thread:** | Black or olive |
| **Tail:** | Olive marabou |
| **Underbody:** | 6-8 wraps medium lead wire |
| **Body:** | Olive Leech Yarn |

**Tying Note:** Leech Yarn has lots of spiky fibers similar to guard hairs so that hackle is not needed. I weight the fly forward of where the thorax of a nymph would begin, to help balance the fly so it tracks level as it's stripped. I tie the marabou about as long as the hook shank to allow it to move sinuously behind the fly. The gills of the natural, which the tail of a damsel pattern imitates, aren't as long but the "swimming" action of this tail gets the job done.

### Mountain Midge

Midges are a mainstay of a mountain trout's diet. The following is a pupa pattern that is easy to tie and easy to vary in color.

| | |
|---|---|
| **Hook:** | Size 18-22 94840, or equivalent |
| **Thread:** | Black |
| **Rib:** | Fine gold wire |
| **Body:** | Black, olive, tan or brown Wee-wool |
| **Hackle:** | Herl |

**Tying Note:** 8/0 Midge thread is thinner for tying with small hooks. Use two or three turns of herl; on small hook use fine herl from the "eye" of a peacock tail feather. Wet wool body midges before you cast so they will drop through the surface film.

## BUYING READY-MADE FLIES

Here is my "A" list of standard commercially available dry flies recommended for the High Sierra. These are high-floating patterns you can rely on in addition to the patterns described above: 12-16 Olive, Tan or Brown Elk Hair Caddis; 14-18 Adams Irresistible; 12-14 Royal, Grey or Grizzly Wulff; 10-18 Yellow, Black or Red Humpy; 18-20 Griffith's Gnat; 16-18 Mosquito; 14-16 Renegade.

My "A" list of standard commercially available wet and nymph patterns is: 12-16 Partridge & Yellow, Partridge & Pheasant, or Partridge & Herl Soft-hackles; 12-16 Zug Bug; 12-18 Gold Ribbed Hare's Ear (natural, olive or black); 12-18 Pheasant Tail Nymph. I typically use weighted nymphs or bead-head versions to get them down to the level where the naturals are found crawling or drifting near bottom.

Other standard commercially available dry flies consistently good for the High Sierra are: 16 PMD or Parachute PMD; 12-16 Red Quill (a.k.a. Mahogany Dun); 14 Little Yellow Stone; 10-12 Kings River Caddis; 14-16 Henryville Special; 12-14 Rio Grande King; 14-18 Adams or Adams Parachute; 14-16 Blue Wing Olive; 16-20 Black Gnat; 12-16 Light Cahill; 14-20 Blue Dun; 12-14 H&L Variant; 10-14 Black Fur Ant or Red Flying Ant; 12-16 Black or Green Foam Beetle; 10-12 Joe's Hopper.

Other standard commercially available wet and nymph flies consistently good for the High Sierra are: 12-14 Prince Nymph; 10-14 Peeking Caddis; 12-14 Bird's Nest; 16-20 Mosquito Larva (Pupa); 10-12 Black, Golden or Olive AP Nymph; 10-12 Montana Nymph; 12-16 Lead Wing Coachman; 12-16 Hare's Ear Wet; 12-16 Dark Cahill Wet; 12-16 Professor; 14-16 Olive, Tan or Orange Scud; 10-12 Black or Olive Woolly Worm or Woolly Bugger; 10-12 Muddler Minnow.

If I had a limited budget, couldn't find anyone to tie the patterns described above and had to choose a basic set of commercial flies (minding the ditty—one for the rock, one for the tree, one for the little fishy), it would include three of each of the following patterns in these sizes:

**Barbless Dry Flies:** 10 Black Foam or Wool Ant; 12 Yellow Humpy; 14 Adams Irresistible; 16 Olive Elk Hair Caddis; 18 Griffith's Gnat.

**Barbless Nymphs & Wet Flies:** 12 Gold Ribbed Hare's Ear; 14 Partridge and Yellow Soft-hackle; 16 Zug Bug; 20 Black Midge Pupa; 12 Olive Woolly Worm or Woolly Bugger.

These reflect my preferences and experience. Your friends and other fly-fishers you ask about flies certainly will have opinions about which is "best." But this set of flies can be relied upon to catch fish "for sure" and any fly shop or mail order or Internet store will carry them.

## FLY BOXES

To carry your flies you will need a fly box. In fact you should carry two in case one is lost or damaged. If you don't already have a fly box, I recommend two clear plastic six-compartment boxes. A small box will hold about 18 size 12 dry flies, more wets. They are inexpensive, durable and importantly, will fit in a standard shirt pocket, unlike many specialty fly boxes. Mix up the wets and drys between the boxes so you don't lose all of one type if you lose a box. Fly boxes and leader spools tend to jump around in your pockets as you are moving through brush and up and down rocks. In the excitement of casting to or playing fish you might not realize your fly box or leader spool fell out. That's a good reason to pick a shirt with roomy button-down flap pockets for your fishing shirt.

Be aware that your hooks can corrode if put away wet. A rusty hook is weak and also stains the dubbing. To avoid this, I drill a few 3/32'ds holes in my plastic fly boxes to allow air to circulate. If I have several wet flies from a particular box, back at camp I will find a sunny spot sheltered from the wind and open the lid to air it out for an hour or so. I will also leave the boxes open overnight after I return to be sure everything dries out before storage.

Getting to the lake basins, hanging canyons and high cirques of the glacier-sculpted High Sierra to fish sapphire lakes for golden trout is what the next chapter is all about.

# Chapter 11

# The Big Lug: Planning a Trip, a Few Words about Gear, and a Surefire Bear Hang

*Here was a lonely universe, eye-blinding with the glare of reflected light but chill with altitude. Nude mountains circled the horizon against the steel-like sky.*

– *Charles McDermand*

*I* am essentially a backpack angler. The pack station operators are as dedicated to the resource as anyone and many people prefer the adventure of horse packing. But I like to focus on the fishing once I get to the mountains with a minimum of distractions and caring for stock is a major distraction. I expect to remain a backpacker until age or injury prevents it. Then I might re-consider horse packing. This chapter is meant for the backpacking angler.

## PLANNING, CAMPING AND CAMPFIRE RESTRICTIONS

Planning a trip to the High Sierra is not difficult. There are well-constructed and maintained trails leading to points within a mile or so of 80% of all lakes and streams in the High Sierra. There are many good books describing the major trails, several of which are included in the bibliography on page 93. There are good books about basic backpacking, several of which are also mentioned in the bibliography. Mountaineering stores and some fly shops carry maps and books. Information about available maps and a list of mail, telephone and Internet sources for maps are included in Appendix A.

## WHEN TO GO

The snow pack is the backbone of High Sierra angling, because clean, cold water is the foundation for fabulous fishing. But it can be a major frustration as well. In heavy snow years there may be accumulations of ten or more feet of unstable snow in the approaches to high passes such as Brown Bear Pass in Emigrant Wilderness or Silver Pass in John Muir Wilderness. It can last well into June and hard-pack snow is usually present well into July. By contrast, in a low snow year, even high passes can be crossed in mid-June if you are willing to kick a few steps in the snow to get over the saddle.

*Paintbrush.*

Late-spring snow storms can occur but are not common. What accounts for the lingering snow is the chilling effect of high altitude. Despite clear skies and bright sun, the snow can be slow to melt down and some of it persists as small glaciers under many peaks year around. Fortunately, the melt advances rapidly below 8000 feet by late May. As a rough guide for the "average" snow year, the June 15 demarcation line above which snow can be an obstacle to travel, is 9000 feet. By the Fourth of July, it is 10,000 feet and by mid-July the high passes should be snow-free except for patches lingering on shaded, north-facing slopes. Roll the dates forward 15 days in a low snow year and roll the dates back 15 days in a deep snow year.

Hard-pack snow is not that difficult to travel over. If snow is covering a scree slope, the snow may provide better footing than the loose rock underneath. But there are several common risks. The snow tends to cover up the trail making route-finding difficult, especially in the woods or when crossing open fell fields with few landmarks. Walking over snow covering talus or other rocky substrate, a boot can punch through the crust and be caught in the rocks, causing a fracture. The glare of reflected sunlight crossing snowfields can damage the eyes and sear unprotected skin. Unless you can confirm the route is passable, it is probably best not to try a route over 9500 feet before July unless you have someone in your party with prior mountaineering experience over snow.

The prime time in the High Sierra is July, August and September, and into October in the south end of the range. Clear to partly cloudy skies, cool nights and warm days are typical of the weather. Occasional thunderstorms pass through, and there is a possibility of snow flurries and cold "snaps" at high elevation even in summer. While it's common sense to get the weather forecast before you leave, severe weather is exceptional in my experience.

Mosquitoes are another story. They will be a serious nuisance from June until mid-August. With the snow melt, the scourge advances with altitude. They take a few days to hatch after the ponds warm, so that the swarm lifts off a week or so after the snow is gone. It's not uncommon to hike right through the hatch on the way to the high country in early season, finding sanctuary only above treeline. Mosquitoes love damp, brushy and woody areas. Choose open dry campsites that receive the evening breeze and are away from water and wet meadows if you want any relief. DEET-based repellant is the best. I carry a spray for my hat and hair or other hard-to-cover areas, and a stick or lotion for exposed skin.

## PLANNING THE TRIP

Consult a trail guide book or similar resource to find an area that interests you. Then, once you have a general area in mind, begin your map research. Start with the three-map series covering the John Muir Wilderness and Sequoia Kings Canyon National Park high country, published by the United States Department of Agriculture Forest Service, or similar maps for other High Sierra wilderness areas, such as Ansel Adams

*Meadow trail.*

Wilderness. See Appendix A. These maps are a bargain, cover almost all of the High Sierra, show the trails, have much helpful information printed on the back and, most importantly, show where there are camping and campfire restrictions.

## GO LEGAL

When I started backpacking there were few restrictions, but the increasing number of people using the wilderness for recreation, and the beauty and easy access to some areas, have made regulations necessary. For the most part, these are intended to mitigate the effects of the "bad habits" of the past, such as cutting wood or camping and grazing stock near water, that prevailed before the "leave no trace" ethic for wilderness camping was practiced. Some are aesthetic as well. Campfires, especially those built up with stones against a large rock, are unsightly and the charcoal and smoke stains on the rocks take a very long time to weather away. (Paleo-archaeologists can locate and date campsites over 10,000 years old just from the charcoal left behind.) Even more important, campfires use up too much wood and woody debris at high elevation, where it is scarce. The decay of fallen logs and branches is essential to building soil and to the life cycle of many plants, insects, animals and birds of the High Sierra. Not only is it the law, but there are good ecological reasons for the Forest Service's camping and campfire restrictions. Thus an important part of your planning will be finding

out what's legal at your destination lake or lake basin. At a minimum, you will need to obtain a campfire/wilderness permit, site your camp 100 feet away from lakes and streams, avoid camping or building a fire where it is illegal and pack out your trash.

## MAP WORK

When planning a trip it is my practice to start with the large scale map, go next to a wilderness or 15-minute topographical map and finally a 7.5-minute (small scale) U.S.G.S. topographical map covering the lakes I want to fish. There is a great deal of extra detail in a 7.5-minute map, and that's the map I most want in my pocket on the trip. I transfer from the larger scale maps any camping, campfire or other legal restrictions. I also note what type of trout can be expected in the lakes using information from California Department of Fish and Game personnel or publications, the charts in Ralph Cutter's *Sierra Trout Guide* (see Bibliography) or by calling the Forest Service or Park Service fisheries biologist for that area. I add trail mileages worked out from the map legend or copied over from commercial maps. I also check and correct trail routes, by comparing newer maps. The last thing I do, because 7.5-minute topos are paper, is to treat the modified topo map with spray "fixer" from an art store. This coats the map with a thin acrylic film which helps protect the map and preserve the added markings.

# Time-to-Distance Planning

The next step is working out the logistics of time. Planning for time is as important as planning for food, matches, what flies to take and so on. In fact it's the basis for your overall decision making. There are five time elements: (1) road travel to the trailhead; (2) trail hiking to your destination; (3) layover time on site; (4) trail hiking back to the trailhead; and (5) road travel back home.

If you are driving from the coastal urban centers of California, it will take at least a half day to drive to a High Sierra trailhead. Often it takes longer; do not be fooled by a large-scale road map. Mountain roads take extra time to travel. And if the trailhead is off the paved road, get a Forest Service base map (see Appendix A) and work out both the route and true mileage in order to plan the travel time. National Forest roads are marked with a letter and number system, not street signs, and unless you carefully memorize the roads and turnoffs, it's asking to get lost if you try to find remote trailheads without taking the map along.

Many people need to acclimate to higher elevation. The best method in my experience is simply to sleep over a night at 6 or 7,000 feet elevation, before hiking in. Taking account of both travel time and acclimation, it's best to plan for one of these alternatives: 1) if you can arrive by noon, a first night's camp at a lake or stream near the trail head; or 2) staying overnight at a Forest Service campground near the trail head before getting a morning start on the trail.

There may be an area for camping at the trail head, but that's an exception. At least, I've not often seen what I'd consider a quality campsite near one. Usually, it's a dusty road end crowded with vehicles that has no water. Walking even a mile up the trail and making a rough camp will beat hanging around the parking area if you get there late.

Based on over twenty years experience at this, I estimate trail time on the following formula: two and one half miles an hour on a moderate trail, two miles an hour on a steep trail, one and one half miles an hour on a very steep trail or cross country, and add a half hour if you will cross a pass, going uphill. Going downhill, add one mile an hour on moderate or steep trails; very steep trails and cross country are about the same downhill with a full pack. Remember to add ten minutes or so per hour for rest stops. This time-to-distance calculation assumes the hiker is in good shape and carrying a pack of 1/3 body weight. It's a good idea to plan a route so you don't have to carry a full pack more than three hours without a long break, and not more than six hours per day. You may be able to go farther faster on the trail, but if that doesn't happen the schedule is "blown" for the rest of the trip. It's better to plan travel time for a chosen route with this "doable" formula.

*Titan's table.*

You can work out how steep the trail will be either from a trail book which describes the elevation gain and loss, or directly from a map using the contour lines. These represent either 40, 60 or 80 feet of elevation change per line, depending on the scale of the map. The legend will spell this out. A trail segment printed where it passes over tightly-spaced contour lines means the trail is steep, very steep if the interval is 80 feet. A segment drawn so it passes over widely-spaced contour lines means the actual trail is more moderate, almost flat if they are far apart and it's a 40-foot interval. Reading the map carefully and working out the difficulty of the trail is a good but inexact planning method. For example, a trail may have features like sandy stretches or a lot of small gullies that don't show on the map, but will slow you down when you actually hike over it. Wet fords of creeks, especially in the early season, will also slow you down. (In early season during high water they can be extremely dangerous—think with your head, not your gonads, in deciding whether to attempt a crossing.) It's best to err on the side of allowing too much time than too little on the first trip over a given trail. The worst that could happen if you overestimate will be to get there sooner and have more time for fishing or other activities, like a refreshing swim on arrival.

After choosing a destination and working out how much time it will take to drive to the trailhead and then hike in, you can complete your plans based on the time you have available. Work out how much food you need by adding layover days to your hiking days, and multiplying by three. I add one extra day's meals as a contingency. Knowing the length of the trip will also help you plan the amount of gear you will need.

The amount and type of gear to carry will depend in part on personal preferences, but also on length of stay and time of year. You will need warmer clothing and water-resistant boots and jacket early and late in the season. An extended trip calls for at least one change of shirt, socks and underclothing, and so on.

If you are going with a buddy or in a small group, your planning should include sharing gear, especially items such as tents and stoves. This reduces redundancy and the total weight to be carried in. "You carry this and I'll carry that" is something to agree on before you go. So is a division of labor for camp chores. Otherwise mutiny and resentment will rule the campsite no matter how good the fishing is.

The last very important consideration is that working out the planning for your intended destination in detail may mean you have to change the plan. If you have a time budget of say, five days, you may find that isn't enough time to hike in and enjoy two days fishing at a lake you have heard about. Or, you might find that a particular route is very steep, and the length of the trip requires a heavy pack, so that it isn't as desirable as it sounded at first. I'm not saying it's never OK to challenge yourself. But it could avoid injury or even death to be realistic about your limits and the limits of others who may be hiking with you. Stay within your limits. After all, the objective is to have fun and catch a few wild trout, not to take unnecessary risks.

*Royce Lakes.*

## HYDRATION, FATIGUE AND FILTERING WATER

There are rich scenic and angling rewards for lugging a backpack uphill, but it is hard, sweaty work. Few backpackers, in my experience, stay hydrated enough for the exertion they are putting out. Summer temperatures in the High Sierra, especially on rocky unshaded slopes, can easily exceed 80 degrees in the afternoon. Doing hard work in summer heat is not the time to cheat your body of water.

One common symptom of dehydration is leg cramps. If you're in good physical condition you won't have leg cramps merely from lugging a pack. If you begin to cramp stop, rest and hydrate well before moving on. You will notice rapid relief from the cramps as soon as you start drinking enough.

Another common symptom is excessive fatigue. If you are in good physical condition, and keep a moderate pace, you won't become exhausted merely from lugging a pack. Being weary from the exertion is one thing. Exhaustion, the listless feeling that you can't go another step, flopping down too tired to take off the pack, etc., is another. It is a symptom of what I call dehydration fatigue. Again, stopping, resting and taking fluids is the remedy. It's a common mistake to try to compensate with sweet, salty "gorp" or other snacks. That's not what your body needs if you are dehydrated. Wait until you are hydrated, then eat a small amount if you actually feel hungry. What you thought was hunger will probably go away as your thirst is slaked. For sure you will be surprised at how fast your energy level picks up again as soon as you are re-hydrated.

People's water needs vary. When I was young, tough and ignorant, I would carry no more than a quart

*Mid-day meditation.*

and made that "stretch." But then, in those days, I didn't hesitate to dip a cup in the small creeks that crossed the trails. I wouldn't do that now. The fact that the water is running and appears clear doesn't mean it's safe to drink. There could be a deer carcass or pile of mule manure in the creek bed around the first bend. I filter my water. Modern filters are fast and effective against common Sierra parasites such as *Giardia*. Filtering water is a minor but necessary inconvenience.

## BOOTS & BLISTERS

Sturdy and supportive boots are essential gear for anyone venturing into the High Sierra. When I started backpacking the choice was either "waffle stompers" or heavy mountaineering boots. A seemingly endless variety of boots are now available, many claiming to fill a special niche, such as trail running, day hiking, heavy trail hiking, backpacking, technical mountaineering and so on. Having walked in the gamut, from mountaineering boots to ultra-light canvas & suede hikers, I can offer a few suggestions for selecting boots.

First, support means essentially an over-the-ankle boot, about 6 inches high for guys, 5 inches for women. I have found that most boots designed for hiking offer plenty of ankle support, whether all leather or nylon canvas and leather "uppers." But many boots are not suitable for the rough, rocky trails of the High Sierra despite a good ankle wrap. Some are outright frauds, having bulky molded "rubber" soles that look impressive but will leave your feet tired and sore.

What's needed is a boot with a sole that has both "torsional control" and is firm enough to protect the foot from stones. Torsional control is a fancy way of saying "resists twisting." A soft-soled boot doesn't protect the foot from the repeated shock of tramping over mile after mile of rocky trail carrying extra weight.

But in the store, how do you avoid a boot that appears rugged but will let you down on the trail? I've devised a couple of simple tests to determine if it will hold up on rocky trails. If you don't have strong hands, you may want to take a friend along who does to do these tests.

The first is the torque test. To test the boot, grip the boot by the heel with one hand and the toe by another and try to twist the shoe in opposite directions. If the sole doesn't resist your twist, and if you can turn the toe more than about 20 degrees, it will tend to flex too much in action.

The second test is what I call the thumb test. Gripping the heel with the other hand, use your dominant hand to grip the front of the boot, holding the fingers over the toe and placing the thumb at the point where the forefoot will flex when walking in the boot. (That's the wide spot just forward of the arch.) Push the thumb up against the middle of the sole to see if you can bend the sole inward. If you can push it in, pass it up since carrying a load it will not protect the foot from stones on a rough trail.

Most so-called day-hikers will fail both of these tests. They may be OK for casual hiking without a pack on groomed trails, and many are otherwise well made. But they aren't the real McCoy. On the other hand, as a kind of bonus, you often find boots priced and marketed as day-hikers that have soles that will easily pass these tests. If the upper boot is well made, they will be OK for backpacking even if they lack the weight and weighty price tag of designated mountaineering boots.

Typically, your regular street shoe size will fit when selecting a boot. If the boot otherwise appeals to your feet, the fit can be fine-tuned using variable thickness insoles (thicker insoles if the boot fits loose, and thinner if it was too tight). You can find both name brand and "generic" insoles for this purpose. Although modern computer-designed boots may seem to be hikeable right out of the box, it's essential to do several miles walking in any new boots to wear them in before taking on a steep trail with a pack.

Blister prevention begins with boots that fit, but socks play an important role. Wearing a thin liner sock (polypropylene fabric works very well) under a thicker sock is good insurance against blisters since the liner sock allows the foot to slide and reduces chafing inside the boot. Dampness inside the boot, which softens the skin, is the prime culprit in blister formation. A wicking liner sock does double duty in also helping to keep the skin dry. If you are blister prone, a trick that really works is to spray your feet with an aluminum-based underarm anti-perspirant for several days before you go, and re-apply each day on the trail, to help keep the skin dry.

The sensation of a blister forming is usually a "hot" spot where the foot is getting chafed. Don't ignore it. Stop right away and remove the boot to check the foot. Cover the hot area with a product called moleskin, which will protect the affected area and has a slick outer surface that will slide. If the skin is already softened or blistering, a good-quality Band-Aid of a size to cover it is better since the pad won't stick to the soft skin. A strip of surgical tape will help hold a Band-Aid in place. It's a good idea to add a "blister kit" composed of a travel-size anti-perspirant, moleskin, Band-Aids and surgical tape to your pack. Even though I very seldom have a blister, I always carry the latter three items on my trips.

## PACKS, CLOTHING AND OTHER GEAR

Despite the hype of the manufacturers and backpacking stores and catalogues, backpacking is not about fashion nor is it a technological race. Once you are in the mountains, all you will care about is comfort and function, and no one is going to pay much attention to your gear, assuming anyone not in your group is even around. A starting backpacker ought to haunt closeout sales, garage sales and thrift stores for gear and clothing. To evaluate what you find, start with the label. It's a fair assumption that the products of the major outdoor manufacturers or vendors were state-of-the-art when first designed, built of quality components and thus likely to be durable.

## BACKPACKS

The first choice is whether to go with an external-frame or internal-frame pack. I own both types and favor the external-frame pack for most purposes in summer hiking.

But if I am planning a trip that includes off-trail hiking, especially over Class II or III ground, I will take an internal-frame pack. An internal-frame pack is less likely to shift weight and throw you off balance on irregular ground, since the weight is held closer to the body. On the other hand, an external-frame pack is a lot cooler to hike in and it's far easier to rig various items such as rod tubes to the frame.

The next decision point is load capacity, usually expressed in cubic inches. Internal-frame packs have greater capacity since the sleeping bag and tent go inside the bag. An external-frame pack lists a smaller capacity since the sleeping bag and tent are typically lashed to the top or bottom of the frame. In comparing the payload of external- and internal-frame packs, you need to deduct for the space taken up by sleeping bag and tent in an internal-frame model.

A net cargo space of 2500 cubic inches is enough for five days of food and gear, in my experience. Three-thousand to 3400 cubic inches can handle up to two weeks since long trips take more food, not a lot more gear. Over 3400 cubic inches is an expedition pack for extended trips. While only my impression, more gear can be loaded onto an external-frame pack despite nominal equal capacity.

Fit is an important matter. Packs come in different sizes and are adjustable. Some store clerks know what

*French Canyon.*

they are doing, others do not. Before you rely on them to adjust a pack, find out what their experience level is generally, and specifically with the product in which you are interested. Ask for a manager and find out his or her qualifications as well if you lack confidence in the salesperson.

Next, try on the pack. The straps should wrap comfortably over the shoulders, from a point level with or just above shoulder height. The hip belt, which will carry the load, should adjust so it rides comfortably across the hip bones (not high at the waist or so low you can't reach into your front pant pocket). It should also adjust so nothing is prodding you in the back or banging into the back of your head. Once you've gotten it adjusted, and you think you might like the pack, load it up with something heavy (at least 25 pounds). Carry it around the store for a few minutes to see how well it handles the load and how much you have to readjust straps and belt. If it still feels OK after you've carried some weight around, start again with another brand or model, before you make a final choice. Try at least two, to get an idea of how they differ and what your preferences seem to be. You may find superficially similar packs feel very different once they are loaded up and worn for even ten minutes or so.

## CLOTHING

When I started out, I thought nothing of heading out with only a couple of cotton tee-shirts, a wool shirt, and a pair of blue jeans. I've learned a lot since then and recommend taking advantage of several new products.

The first thing I've learned is the layering system works. The number one, two, three and four upper layers that are essential for the High Sierra are a wicking undershirt, mosquito-proof long-sleeve shirt for camp and fishing wear, a lightweight wind-shell garment for windy days, and a wool or fleece sweater for cool nights. What to carry beyond that is often a matter of personal preference but I can offer a few thoughts.

The so-called wicking fabrics are a truly worthwhile innovation. These garments are very lightweight and can keep you both warm and cool, depending on the weather. Their breathe-ability and lack of absorbency are the key. Worn alone, they are cool. Worn as a base layer under outer layers, they keep the skin dry (the wicking part) and free of evaporative heat loss. The original fabric, still very effective, is polypropylene (polypro). The only drawback to polypro is that it holds odors; later versions are treated to retard bacterial growth and minimize this drawback.

*Camping under Foxtails.*

HIGH SIERRA FLY FISHING • BASICS TO ADVANCED TACTICS

I generally carry both a short-sleeve wicking shirt and a long-sleeve wicking shirt and pants set as a thermal layer. The tee-shirt can be worn alone or under another layer. The backup set is very compact and will yield a very high thermal advantage for its slight weight if ever needed. I also carry a watchcap and gloves in a "ditty bag" with this set early or late in the year.

An "open-weave" or "pique" shirt or standard flannel shirt won't be mosquito-proof. A wool or heavy weight twill or canvas weave cotton shirt with flap pockets for fly boxes is better. A good wool shirt can often be found at thrift stores if you are on a budget. Nylon fishing shirts are sturdy, lightweight and the "flats" type has big pockets, but they offer no warmth after the sun goes down. If I carry one, I carry it in addition to a heavier shirt.

A wind shell should be of the stuffs-in-its-own-pocket or -bag type. This makes it easy to stow when not in use and to carry along when you are away from camp hiking or fishing. It's a good idea to put your wind shell on after hiking up to a windy lake at high altitude; you could chill down rapidly to the point of hypothermia in a sweat-wet shirt at a breezy lake. A basic "rip stop" nylon wind shell is inexpensive and all you will really need. I prefer the anorak or pull-over type, but also have used the zip-front style.

Most people bring an outer thermal layer. Down vests and jackets are popular. A wool-lined parka is popular with some hikers. I have found they are not very portable for fishing or day hiking, though. A jacket with a fabric shell and a removable polyester fleece liner is versatile and very popular. The drawback is bulk. Fleece just doesn't compress very much, so these garments tend to take up a disproportionate amount of space. You can get the same thermal effect with a wind shell and wool sweater. I find that a sweater and a fleece or down vest are all the thermal layers that I routinely need.

One last layer to consider is rainwear of some kind. For many years I've carried a lightweight poncho, but only actually needed it twice. I have friends who have been rained on and even snowed on, and so lug a full rain suit around. As I see it, if you are carrying a tent, you are unlikely to need full rain gear. Most of the dark clouds I've encountered in the High Sierra in summer spit out a few fat drops and moved on, without even managing to wet down the trail dust. In the event of serious wet weather or snow, make camp and set up the tent. Your tent will provide far better protection than the finest of rain gear. Summer storms rarely last long in the High Sierra, and you will soon be getting back to business.

Whether to wear shorts or pants is a matter of personal preference. If you prefer hiking in shorts, a backup pair of pants should be in the pack. If the weather turns cool or you hike through brushy country, the pants will better protect your legs. I prefer six-pocket cargo pants, either twill or canvas weave. I also carry nylon wind pants to mate with my wind shirt.

Granite is abrasive. The wear point of pants or shorts after many sits tends to be the fabric between the back pockets. To ensure durability, I wear pants made of

*Whitebark detail.*

8-ounce cotton fabric. Nylon fabric is OK, but it will still abrade in the same spot and is more difficult to patch. The advantages of nylon are that it dries very quickly (say after wading a creek) and untreated nylon pants (the "river runner" type) are breathable and cool to walk in.

## STOVES

A cooking stove is essential, since campfires are not allowed above 9000 feet in most of the High Sierra. I use an LP/butane mix gas stove because the fuel burns soot-free, can't spill, and the stove is simpler and less prone to damage or malfunction than the liquid fuel type. But the latter stoves have legions of fans, albeit they spend a lot of time "fine-tuning" in camp. White gas burns hotter and thus boils water faster—slightly faster—than butane. For me the slight difference is well worth avoiding the risk of gasoline leaking on my food or clothes in the pack.

LP and butane gas are sold in pressurized metal cans that plug or screw into the stove. You will have to pack out empties as a result. White gas is typically transferred to a reusable aluminum bottle for backpacking, which also has to be carried out. So the convenience of carrying either fuel is pretty much a trade-off. White gas, which can be purchased in quantity, is cheaper than LP or butane gas cans.

*Foxtail pine.*

It can be tricky to plan for fuel, since low temperatures and other variables, such as food selection and wastage, will affect fuel consumption. As a rough guide, assume you will be bringing one and one-half liters of water to a roiling boil for three minutes twice a day. The instructions on the fuel-can label will tell you the manufacturer's claimed boil rate and burn time, from which you can calculate how many you will need. For example, a fuel can might state it will bring 15 liters of water to a boil. Obviously, it is better to overestimate by a day or so than underestimate your fuel.

---

**About Boiling Water**

Boiling water for three minutes will kill *Giardia*. But using filtered water to cook with uses a lot less fuel, since you will only need to heat water for beverages or bring it to a boil momentarily to prepare freeze-dried foods.

---

## SLEEPING BAGS

A mummy-style bag with a thermal rating of 10 to 25 degrees is a good choice for summer camping in the Sierras. Excellent synthetic sleeping bags are available these days for less than a hundred dollars for someone on a limited budget.

There are two things to keep in mind in selecting a sleeping bag. First, the temperature ratings are made by the manufacturer and are influenced by salesmanship. A bag rated at 15 degrees by one manufacturer may suspiciously have the same weight of the same fill material as a bag rated by another manufacturer at 20 degrees. If you are a "cold" sleeper, choose a bag at the next lower temperature rating. Second, as a general matter, a warmer bag takes more fill and will be both heavier and bulkier.

The next decision is whether to go with synthetic or down filling. Synthetic fillings are excellent insulators and offer some cushioning underneath. Synthetics will insulate when wet, but no bag insulates to its dry rating wet. They do have the drawback that they do not compress as much as down.

I own a goose down bag and sometimes use it. And I know of many who swear by them for their high warmth-to-weight ratio in the Sierras, which lack the humidity and wet weather of the Cascades or Alaska. The trouble is, down takes extra care in the field to avoid getting it wet and it takes special cleaning and storage or it loses all its advantages. If you have a choice, start with a synthetic fill bag.

## TENTS

I scoffed at carrying a tent for many years, taking along only a 5x7 tarp as a ground cloth. Even now I often go solo with only a summer-weight bivy sack. But there are so many very good, lightweight and inexpensive backpacking tents it has become a buyer's market of sales and discounts.

What you want is a so-called "three season" tent, which will be a tent consisting of an under tent and cover called a "fly." Any good-quality tent will be easy to set up, have basic privacy and provide protection from the elements and mosquitoes. (Note the last is the principal use of a tent in the Sierra Nevada in mid-summer.) Virtually all tents are made of cut sheets of coated nylon fabric so (despite the hype) the differences are largely a matter of convenience.

Here's what it's about: Free-standing means the tent has poles that bend into hoops that fit into grommets at the corners and hold it up without needing tent stakes. A few models assemble into an A-frame the tent is draped over. Non-free-standing means the tent has poles or hoops in the middle but needs the ends staked down to stand up.

Free-standing tents are heavier for a given floor area than non-free-standing tents, since they typically have more poles, longer poles and more surface area than a non-free-standing tent. A few tents in the lower price range are still offered with fiberglass poles; most tents have aluminum poles. Fiberglass poles are heavier than aluminum poles, and fell out of favor when they failed under stress at very low temperatures on a few expeditions. There are manufacturers that offer the same tent with aluminum poles as one model and fiberglass poles as another, at a substantially lower price. Fiberglass poles are perfectly OK for a summer tent for the High Sierra if you are on a budget. You compare tents by "carry" or total weight. Note some manufacturers try to make their tents seem light by only listing the "tent" weight without adding in stakes, etc., and that's a hint they might be cutting other corners.

Because they rely on tension from the stakes, non free-standing tents tend to be designed with a narrow rectangular floor shape; free-standing tents tend to be polygonal or "dome" shaped, and thus wider across. There are trade offs in both designs, a narrow profile cheats the wind sited into a prevailing wind but a dome-shape sheds gusts in cross-winds. The advantage of a free-standing tent is that it can be set up on solid granite. A non-free-standing tent needs soil or gravel to plant the stakes. An advantage of non-free-standing tents is that front and rear vestibules are larger than those of most dome tents.

Use both tent styles. While I'll generally trade a little inconvenience for lighter weight, a lot depends on the model. I can't strongly recommend one type over the other. Most stores have samples set up on the sales floor, so you can see what you get for your money.

## A Surefire Bear Hang

A visit from a bear is uncommon in the High Sierra above the sub-alpine pine belt, in my experience at least. But in the pine belt on the approach trail, especially in National Parks, you could lose your entire food supply and your pack in the process. Bears are smart and quickly learn about the high nutrition found in packs.

The basic technique for avoiding bear damage is to hang food bags in a tree at night or when you are away from your camp. Hanging your food clear of any trees is the key. Sierra bears can climb a tree and out on a limb to get at the bags. You can get a bag pretty high just tossing a rope over the end of a high limb and hauling the bag up. But the rope has to be tied off and some bears know about this. They will pull on the rope until it breaks or the bag pulls down.

The Forest Service sometimes provides a steel cable between two trees to hang food. A similar set-up can be rigged with a rope stretched between two trees. You don't need the perfect limb, just two trees at least fifteen feet apart. You will also need better rope than parachute cord. At a mountaineering store ask for 75 to 100 feet of 4 to 6 mm "zip" cord. This is a braided, high-strength, climbing type rope. You will also need to learn another fishing knot, the dropper loop.

The basic step is to select two trees to suspend the rope between. Tie a rock to the end of the rope and toss it over a stout limb near the trunk 15 feet high. Pull the rope over the limb and wrap the rope around the trunk clockwise three wraps and tie off snugly. Pull the other end to draw the line tight. Next tie one or more dropper loops in the rope, at points that will clear any branches once suspended. Tie a rock to the remaining rope end and toss it over a stout limb near the trunk at the right height in the second tree. Tie on a bag and pull the line tight between the trees. Check to be sure the loop is far enough out to be clear of branches, preferably dead center between the trees. Drop the rope and re-tie your knots if necessary.

When you are ready to hang food, tie the food bags to the loops. If you have several in the party you can tie two bags to the same loop. Use more loops to spread the

weight if there are several bags. Then pull the rope up over the limb of the second tree, hoisting the bags tied to the loops into the air between the trees. If you have done it right the bags will be suspended twelve feet up and at least six feet from any limbs. Then wrap the rope counter-clockwise two or three turns around the second trunk and tie off. The zip cord is strong enough to withstand bear tampering, and the counter-wound rope over bark will resist pulling down. See Figure 4.

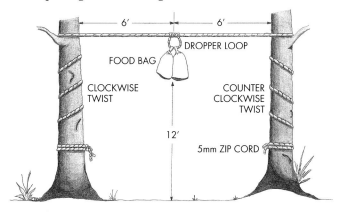

Figure 4. Bear Hang

The dropper loop is easy to learn and is easy to untie when it's time to break camp. Make a loop in the rope. Fold the loop over the doubled part. Repeat that twice more, so there are three twists. Separate the doubled part in the middle, and pull the loop through and tug which will pull the twists tighter. Then pull the rope from both ends until the knot seats, with the loop pinched between the now-coiled twists, three on each side. See Figure 5.

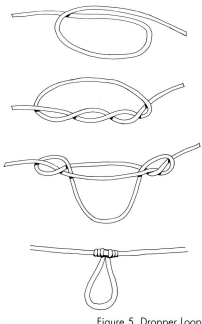

Figure 5. Dropper Loop

It is a very good idea, if you have to camp in an area with "educated" bears, to site the tents well away from the bear hang. Because of their excellent sense of smell, keep all snacks, toothpaste, garbage and any scented items hung in the food bags and out of packs and tents at night or when you are away from camp. Tying pots and metal cups to the bags acts as an alarm. If bears show up, put on a "great ape" act of arm waving, throwing rocks, hollering and other noise-making to drive them off. In this game, once the bears get the food you have to let them have it. Don't risk serious injury by trying to get it back.

# Chapter 12

# A Cloud on the Horizon:
# The Future of High Sierra Angling

*The aquatic/riparian systems are the most altered and impaired habitats of the Sierra. . . . Introduction of non-native fishes (primarily trout) has greatly altered aquatic ecosystems through impacts on native fish, amphibians, and invertebrate assemblages.*

*—Executive Summary, Sierra Nevada*

# ECOSYSTEM PROJECT REPORT

The Fish and Game crews tried, but failed, to save the 1949 run. The final effort to salvage the lone remaining year class of San Joaquin spring-run salmon was scheduled in 1950. We knew that if we failed, this unique renewable resource would be lost forever.

—George Warner

There are some clouds on the angler's horizon for the High Sierra. In 1992, with a Congressional mandate, geologists, foresters, biologists and other scientists were assembled to undertake a task that had never been done before—to make a comprehensive survey of the ecology of the Sierra Nevada. Resource managers and others responsible for management of public lands and parks within the Sierra Nevada had concluded that they were essentially "shooting blind" in making many management decisions because they lacked area-wide data about the land and resources. The Sierra Nevada Ecosystem Project (or SNEP) was created to compile the data, taking in an area from the fir forests at the Oregon border to the desert foothills south of Bakersfield, and from the Oak Grasslands of the Gold Country on the west side, to the High Sage Desert below the Eastern Escarpment.

The conclusions of the SNEP Report are important and likely to become a basis for long-term resource planning for many years to come. One of the most encouraging conclusions is that the sub-alpine Sierra forests are vigorous and healthy. There are concerns about air pollution and ozone damage in the southern Sierra (near urban and industrial build-up), periodic pest infestation and plant disease epidemics, and the effects of fire suppression on woodland habitats. Pests, disease and fire are natural processes that ultimately contribute to the health of the forest. Indeed some species, such as the giant sequoia, depend on fire to clear forest openings where seeds can germinate. Allowing pest infestations to run their course, allowing fires to burn away the brushy understory of the forests and woodlands and reducing air pollution and ozone, are obvious if not always easy or expedient solutions to adopt. Despite air pollution in the southern reaches, the overall health of the forest is very encouraging.

There are many different interests at work and play in the Sierra Nevada. Lumber, mining and agriculture, and ever increasingly, recreation and retirement communities, form the economic base of the region. One of the conclusions of the report is that the number of human inhabitants engaged in the lumber, mining and agricultural industries have remained static or declined since 1970, but the total mountain population has more than doubled. The interests of the old economy are often disparate from those of the new, a point addressed in the report.

Of concern to anglers are the public lands that comprise almost all of the High Sierra. In the High Sierra, there is essentially no lumbering, no agriculture except livestock grazing and only a few remnant mining claims. In the High Sierra, recreation is king, and the trout are the kings of the waters. The problem for anglers arises from the argument the trout are usurpers of the aquatic natural order in the High Sierra.

Ironically, the Report points out that the greatest cumulative negative impacts of historic land use in the Sierra Nevada to any fauna have been to fish. Nineteenth century hydraulic mining and more recent dam construction devastated native fish populations. Over 90% of anadromous fish, such as the salmon and steelhead trout of the west slope, or Lahontan cutthroat trout on the east slope, have been exterminated in the Sierra Nevada. For example, after the water was diverted to agriculture in 1948, the last runs of king salmon in the San Joaquin River, which once numbered in the millions, gasped and died. They died in the de-watered riverbed east of Los Banos in the Central Valley, 50 miles from the diversion at Friant Dam, despite the desperate efforts of California Fish & Game personnel to shunt the fish into irrigation canals. All major tributaries except the Consumnes River are now dammed in the Sierra Nevada, some more than once. The prospect for restoration of the runs of anadromous fish in many Sierra Nevada rivers is at best discouraging, and in several cases impossible due to loss of the genetic base.

Resource and conservation issues arise for trout because, contrary to the fate of anadromous trout and salmon at lower elevations, in the High Sierra, trout have vastly expanded their former range. As pointed out in Chapter 1, except for the golden trout of the Kern River plateau and the Paiute cutthroat of the East Walker River drainage, which may have occupied waters as high as 8200 feet, the High Sierra was barren of trout before 1860.

The first despoilers of the High Sierra riparian habitat also became the first trout propagators, when Basques and other Euro-Americans began seasonal stock-grazing of high meadows. Since they spent weeks at a time in the back country with uncertain supply, to supplement their diet the shepherds and stockmen

*Yellow-legged frog.*

began to "seed" the lakes with trout captured from low-elevation streams. These were the so-called "coffee pot" trout plants, named after their favorite means of transport. By 1880 or so there were many high-country lakes bearing trout from these plants, as well as widespread damage to meadows and streams from the grazing, as documented by John Muir and others.

At about that time, both state and federal governments began fish-hatchery programs for stocking trout fry and eggs into High Sierra lakes and streams by mule-train. Later, in the 1940s, it was discovered that fingerling trout could be planted by air and the planting of the high country began in earnest. Almost all of the 4,000 or so lakes in the High Sierra have been planted at least on a trial basis since then, even remote lakes inaccessible by stock. This included both National Forests as well as National Park lands. In the glory days of fish planting, even Yosemite had its own hatchery program complete with big trout derbies.

Starting in the late 1960s and with growing momentum since the 1970s, the National Park Service has re-examined its policies and practices in light of its mandate to preserve park lands in their original condition. This led, among other things, to abolishing such distractions as bear wrestling and fire falls and limiting access to sensitive areas to reduce human impact on popular sites within our National Parks. It also meant strict enforcement of a policy of no exotic (non-native) plants or animals on park lands.

In the case of trout, this has meant an end to in-park hatcheries and a drastic reduction or elimination of trout planting. It has also lead to specific management policies, such as allowing the take of (exotic) brown trout but enforcing catch-and-release of rainbows in Yosemite Valley, with the eventual objective of eradication of the brown. While there is room to argue with this or other methods, in the end, conserving the ecosystem within the parks is a legal mandate and the Park Service will have to comply.

A second strategy, considered by SNEP, is a lot more controversial. That is the reduction or removal of introduced native species of trout, even where they have become established. Trout are at the top of the food chain in most High Sierra waters. (There are other apex predators such as gulls, kingfishers, ospreys and river otters sometimes present in the High Sierra habitat.) As a result trout have a significant effect on the life forms in High Sierra lakes. For example, zooplankton, which graze algae and help keep the water clear, range from microscopic to 2 mm in size in Sierra waters. In many lakes where trout were introduced, the larger zooplankton are essentially extinct due to predation.

A creature known as the yellow-legged frog has become a symbol of sorts for this process. This frog was widespread across the length and breadth of the High Sierra historically. Now it is vastly reduced in population and territory. The prevailing theory holds that predation by planted trout on the tadpoles, which take two to three years to mature in cold, nutrient-poor high-elevation lakes, is the cause. (There has been a worldwide decline in amphibian population, however, which may or may not be due to increased solar radiation due to man-induced atmospheric changes.) With the yellow-legged frog as their example, there are now advocates for removing trout from many lakes to try to restore the original ecosystem.

There is anecdotal angling evidence of the trout's effects on high-lake environments. In his books, Charles McDermand mentions the large average size of the trout. See Bibliography. Many of these were trout that grew rapidly in a prey-rich environment after the High Sierra lakes were first planted. Rose Lake was one water he mentioned. But Rose Lake, since McDermand fished it in the 1940s, has developed a population of pan-sized golden trout as the lake reached a predator-prey equilibrium. See Chapter 3.

Another example is the Wind River Range in Wyoming, where fish-planting began rather late after 1940. World-record cutthroat and golden trout were taken in the early days, weighing as much as 11 pounds. But the average size of the fish has drastically declined in the years since then, as the rich pre-planting food base has been depleted by trout predation.

On the other hand, I know of several areas of the High Sierra that have reached a balance where yellow-legged frogs, salamanders and other aquatic animals co-exist with introduced trout. The Wright Lakes Basin near Mt. Whitney (yellow-legged frog) or Laurel Lake in Yosemite (California newt) come to mind, as examples where trout and amphibians cohabit successfully. And, there are uncounted thousands of tarns, seeps, wet meadows and riparian areas in the High Sierra that won't support trout but clearly provide habitats for both vertebrate and invertebrate species that will never be impacted by trout predation, including plankton and yellow-legged frogs. It is highly unlikely that the trout planted in the High Sierra will cause the extinction of any species except perhaps on a localized basis, in a given lake.

The SNEP report did make several helpful findings, such as the extent to which lakes and other waters were being planted that had self-sustaining populations of trout. Obviously ending such planting is a good idea. It's a waste of money and effort and it repeatedly disrupts the gene pool of trout that have adapted to the High Sierra, or evolved there in the first place, such as the golden trout.

So what are the long-term implications of characterizing trout as an "exotic species" in the High Sierra ecosystem? Will it mean regulating an end to trout fishing in the High Sierra? I think the answer is reasonably clear. Even if you equate conservation or preservation of park and wilderness lands with restoration, there is no going back to the nineteenth century. The land has been too extensively altered, there are too many people claiming a right to the pursuit of happiness in a wilderness setting, and the balance of nature itself has shifted too much since the 'good old days.' The meaning of civilization, in the end, is altering the environment for man's benefit, even if it's as simple as using an inflatable sleeping pad.

More to the point, while there might be an abstract value to knowing the zooplankton are undisturbed in the high lakes, there is considerably more recreation value in angling for trout, not to mention so-called "tourist dollars." Fully 40% of all backcountry visitors place angling high among their objectives. That's a pretty substantial constituency among the citizens actually entering the High Sierra. Certainly their interests are as worthy of consideration as those of the crowds that have their meals served with wine and table cloth inside permanent structures within the shadow of El Capitan, or cruise Cedar Grove over permanent highways in busses spewing clouds of diesel smoke, without even exiting.

What I believe is the best and most practical solution to the often conflicting objectives of providing quality recreation in an unspoiled environment, is to let the Sierra go wild. Manage to conserve, but don't waste time or money on expensive experiments such as mitigating Malakoff Diggings or removing trout from the Recess Lakes. Malakoff Diggings is in the midst of an area remade by nineteenth century hydraulic mining, which literally moved mountains and choked the Feather, Yuba and American rivers with debris. Sensibly, the State of California has made a historic park of the site rather than "fix" it. In the case of trout, removal is impractical. Chemical treatment will harm other species indiscriminately, not just the trout. Mechanical means, such as nets, aren't thorough. It only takes a few escapees to re-populate a given water—after all, not many trout fit into those coffee pots.

The eventual result, as has happened in Yosemite and Sequoia Kings Canyon where the no-plant policy has been in effect the longest, is that the trout die off in waters that won't support them, such as Boundary Lake in Yosemite, but will 'revert' to the wild in other waters where they can survive, such as nearby Kibbie Lake, where they have been present since homesteader Kibbe put a few trout there in 1875.

There are counter-points to the argument that the presence of trout in much of the High Sierra is "unnatural." The golden trout, a subspecies of redband trout and more primitive than the coastal rainbow, evolved in the streams of the Kern plateau because it was isolated from Central Valley rivers and the sea in an unglaciated pocket by a geological accident—a barrier to continued upstream migration. Genetically-pure strains of golden trout persist only because they were transplanted to barren lakes, where they were not subjected to competition and hybridization by rainbow trout in modern times.

Paiute cutthroat, a subspecies of Lahontan cutthroat trout, originally evolved above a barrier falls that collapsed in an earthquake within historic times. The Paiute cutthroat persists as a genetically distinct group

*Caltech Peak.*

only because the sheepherders moved a few pure trout into barren water further upstream, above a second barrier falls. That coffee-pot plant protected them from hybridization after the lower falls were breached. The reason the two sub-species of trout originally present in the High Sierra still exist is that they were transplanted into waters formerly barren.

There are secret lakes in the High Sierra that are a refuge for a cutthroat trout sub-species native to the Rocky Mountains. The cutthroats were acquired by the California Department of Fish and Game in a 1930s "swap" for golden trout and planted in then-barren lakes. Many years later, eggs taken from the trout in those lakes were the basis for restoration of the sub-species in its original waters after it was threatened with extinction. The geographic isolation of the "forgotten" cutthroat trout ensured the survival of their subspecies. The practice of planting remote lakes has since been adopted as a deliberate conservation strategy both in California and in other states seeking to isolate genetic strains of trout. Ironically, the same strategy has been proposed to conserve yellow-legged frogs.

These instances of the conservation of rare subspecies, dictate there would have to be many exceptions even to a formalized eradication plan. Otherwise, the

*Columbine.*

*White fir.*

logical extension of an eradication policy would be to remove Paiute cutthroat from their current refuge above the upper falls, because they were introduced and thus upset the upstream "balance of nature," and to exterminate the foreign cutthroat because they are exotic to the High Sierra.

It is my view that there is neither a "law of nature" nor a compelling moral or aesthetic value that dictates the ecosystem above a falls without trout is inherently "better" than the ecosystem below the falls with trout. In nature such a barrier results from purely physical processes and is subject to change, as with the collapse of the falls that almost sealed the fate of the Paiute cutthroat. The persistence of trout in a watershed where they were originally introduced is a "trace" of mankind's past presence, to be sure. But it is not the sort of trace that results in consequences that could not occur as a result of natural changes, nor one that is ever likely to degrade anyone's wilderness experience in a substantial way. On the contrary, at least 40% of the visitors to the High Sierra think the presence of trout enhances the wilderness experience.

The better approach and the most practical approach is to let nature sort herself out. That implies halting further planting, but it also means not attempting radical retrofitting by trying to remove trout. The ecosystem will adjust itself over time, and wild trout will persist where the Sierra eco-system will accommodate them. They will eventually, inevitably be eradicated where it won't. Short-term population fluctuations of impacted prey species will stabilize and they will become abundant again where the trout decline. In this way the High Sierra ecosystem, like most ecosystems, efficiently self-regulates. The best course is to tinker least with what has become a reality over the last 120 years. The beautiful wild creatures displayed in this book are an integral feature of the granite wonderland of the High Sierra, worthy of conservation in their own right.

# APPENDIX A
## Where to Get Maps And Wilderness Permits

## MAPS

Maps are essential both for planning a trip and to route-finding in the wilderness. A recent innovation is downloading maps from CD ROM disks or the Internet. However, how useful these are depends in substantial part on the quality of your printer and printer paper. Printing out several "chunks" of the territory you want to travel and taping them together is a hassle. So far I can't recommend CDs except as a planning tool. Printed maps (especially those offered on waterproof, tearproof paper) are still the maps to carry along.

The basic maps are the United States Geological Survey (U.S.G.S.) topographical maps, universally called "topo" maps for short. These are carried by backpacking and mountaineering stores throughout California. This is convenient but be aware topo maps covering popular areas tend to sell out, especially during summer months. Don't wait until the last minute or you may have some frantic calling around to do to find the map you need.

If you know which topo maps you want, they can be ordered direct from the U.S.G.S. at:

### U.S. Geological Survey
Federal Center • Box 25286 • Denver, CO 80225

The U.S. Department of Agriculture Forest Service publishes excellent full-color topographical trail maps of designated wilderness areas in their "Guide to" series, including Emigrant Wilderness, Hoover Wilderness, Ansel Adams Wilderness, Golden Trout Wilderness and a three-page map covering the John Muir Wilderness and Sequoia-Kings Canyon back country. Several are available in later editions on waterproof paper and include trail mileage. Surrounding park and wilderness lands are shown and these maps are both highly recommended and inexpensive. The Forest Service also publishes a base map for each of the National Forests that include parts of the High Sierra, including Inyo, Sequoia, Sierra, and Stanislaus national forests. These aren't topos but are especially useful in showing man-made features, including campgrounds and the Forest Service road system that will take you to most trail heads.

U.S. Department of Agriculture Forest Service Pacific Southwest Region office has published a pamphlet entitled "A Guide To National Forest Wilderness in California," that gives an overview of the several National Forest areas in the High Sierra and lists the addresses and phone numbers of the Ranger District offices where permits and local information can be obtained. The Guide and Forest Service wilderness maps can be ordered direct from:

### U.S.D.A. Forest Service Attn: Map Sales
4260 Eight Mile Road • Camino, CA 95709

Or you can simply click Maps at the Pacific Southwest Region website: http://sv0505.r5.fs.fed.us.

There is no sales tax or shipping charge for maps ordered directly from the Forest Service.

There are also several commercial map makers that offer maps of various segments of the High Sierra. Because topo maps are drawn based on survey lines, one map often doesn't include your entire route, leaving off essentials such as the trail head, or may cut a lake or ridge crest in half, and so on. They are accurate only as of the date of publication; later changes such as elevation corrections or trail re-routing are not shown until a map is republished, which can be ten or more years.

The commercial map makers, such as Wilderness Press, have drawn their maps to compensate for these problems, such as providing expanded coverage by including information from adjoining 15-minute topos, or redrawing the topos on a larger scale to include more territory. Because 7.5-minute topos still have the best physical detail, I highly recommend obtaining one covering the environs of your destination lake or peak. See Chapter 11. Some of the commercial map makers have also included trail mileages, and all have updated the trail information on older topos.

The same backpacking and mountaineering stores that carry topos also carry commercial maps and so do the Information Centers at the ranger stations listed below. But they can be ordered directly from the following:

### Wilderness Press Map Center
2440 Bancroft Way • Berkeley, CA 94704
800-282-3963 (Adventurous Traveler Books)
www.wildernesspress.com

Note: The Wilderness Press website includes a bulletin board worth consulting before a trip which contains trail updates and other information pertinent to use of their maps and trail books. The price of Wilderness Press Hiking Guide trail books for popular areas of the Sierra Nevada include a waterproof topo map showing updated trail routes; they fit in a shirt pocket and are a bargain.

### Tom Harrison Cartography
2 Falmouth Cove • San Rafael, CA 94901-4465
800-265-9090 • website: www.tomharrisonmaps.com

Note: Harrison maps are three-color shaded-relief maps that give a three-dimensional effect. They have trail mileage, and 80-foot contour intervals. A new feature is to add a contour elevation index number at trail junctions and campgrounds, so that elevation gain and loss as well as mileage can be worked out from the map. UTM grid coordinates are also included for GPS users.

### National Geographic Maps Trails Illustrated Series
P.O. Box 4357 • Evergreen, CO 80437-4357
800-962-1643 • website: www.trailsillustrated.com

Note: The relevant Trails Illustrated Series maps cover Yosemite and Sequoia-Kings Canyon National Parks. These are waterproof topo maps which include trail mileage.

## WHERE TO GET A WILDERNESS PERMIT

### An Important Trip-Planning Note

There are daily quotas on many popular trailheads and destinations. It is a good idea to call at least four to six weeks ahead to ask about availability and if necessary reserve a permit. In Yosemite and Kings Canyon national parks, read four to six months ahead of time. Although there typically is an allotment of unreserved spaces for walk-ins at many trailheads, it's asking for aggravation to risk precious time off from work or school on the chance of getting a first-come, first-serve permit. If you must go without a reservation, at least call the ranger station and ask for suggestions about what's available. Be flexible and willing to accept a permit for a trail less popular.

More specific information about permits and quotas can be obtained on-line. Reservation, quota and permit information is available at the National Park Service site for Yosemite: http://www.nps.gov/yose/ and for Sequoia Kings Canyon: http://www.nps.seki/. At the Pacific Southwest Region Forest Service site, http://www.r5.fs.fed.us, you can point and click on the displayed map, and quickly obtain detailed information, including current addresses and telephone numbers of ranger stations where wilderness permits are obtained. The Sierra Club also maintains a web site with useful information and links. Go to: http://www.angelschapter.org/sps/trails and click on the wilderness or park in which you are interested.

The following are the ranger stations you are most likely to visit to obtain a permit for the High Sierra:

## A. ALL EASTSIDE TRAILHEADS

### White Mountain Ranger District
789 North Main • Bishop, CA 93514
760/873-2500 • (Middle of town; carry books & maps)

### Mammoth Ranger District
P.O. Box 148 • Mammoth Lakes, CA 93546
760/924-5500
(Turn west off 395 on Mammoth Lakes Dr.; open 7 days)

### Bridgeport Ranger District
P.O. Box 595 • Bridgeport, CA 93517
760/932-7070 • (On 395 south of town)

## B. WESTSIDE TRAILHEADS

## 1. EMIGRANT WILDERNESS AND N. YOSEMITE

### Forest Supervisor's Office Stanislaus National Forest
19777 Greenly Road • Sonora CA 95370
(Off Mono Road. East of Old town)

### Summit Ranger District
1 Pinecrest Lake Road • Pinecrest, CA 95364
209/965-3434
(Off Highway 108 at Dodge Ridge Resort turn-off)

## 2. YOSEMITE NATIONAL PARK

### Groveland Ranger District
24525 Old Highway 120 • Groveland, CA 95321
209/962-7825 • (Off 120, a right eastbound)

### Wilderness Center Yosemite National Park
P.O. Box 545 • Yosemite, CA 95389
209/372-0740
(Note: Yosemite books and maps are available at Curry Village bookstore; a few at Tuolumne store)

## 3. SOUTH YOSEMITE & BEASORE ROAD TRAILHEADS

### Mariposa Ranger District
41969 Highway 41 • Oakhurst, CA 93644
209/683-4665
(A couple miles north of Oakhurst; summer-use-only station at Clover Meadow on Beasore Road)

## 4. EDISON LAKE & FLORENCE LAKE TRAILHEADS

### Pine Ridge Ranger District
P.O. Box 559 • Prather, CA 93651
209/855-5360
(At Highway 168/Auberry Rd. junction; summer only use High Sierra Station on Kaiser Pass Road)

## 5. COURTWRIGHT/WISHON RESERVOIRS TRAILHEADS

### Pineridge Ranger District
P.O. Box 300 • Shaver Lake, CA 93664
209/841-3311
(On west side Highway 168 before Shaver Lake)

## 6. SEQUOIA/KINGS CANYON NATIONAL PARK

### Sequoia Kings Canyon N.P.
Wilderness Permit Reservations
HCR 89 Box 60 • Three Rivers, CA 93271
209/565-3708
($10 fee, must reserve 3 weeks in advance)

## 7. SOUTH SIERRA/DOMELANDS

### Sequoia National Forest
Cannell Meadow Ranger District
P.O. Box 6 • Kernville, CA 93238
760/376-3781 • (105 Whitney Road)

### Greenhorn Ranger District
P.O. Box 3810 • Lake Isabella, CA 93240
760/379-5646 • (4875 Ponderosa Dr.)

# BIBLIOGRAPHY

The following is a list of recommended books and web sites, organized into categories of information that will be of interest to High Sierra anglers, with a few comments about the content. Unless noted, the books are still in print and available. If you are on a budget, some books may be found at your local library or you may be able to find used copies.

## ABOUT THE BIG BLOCK OF ROCK

—*Assembling California*, John McPhee, Farrar, Strous & Giroux (1993). McPhee is a master of prose and manages to weave a fascinating story out of tectonics.

—*Geology of the Sierra Nevada,* Mary Hill, University of California Press (1975). Not a drop of dry boring lecture here. Plenty of juicy mining and other history blended into the story of the rocks. One of my favorites.

—*Sierra Nevada Ecosystem Report* (1996), Sierra Nevada Ecosystem Project. The entire report is accessible on-line or can be ordered from the United States Printing Office in print or CD format: http://ceres.ca.gov/snep or http://alexandria.ucsb.edu/snep. An interagency summary of project information relevant to anglers entitled "High Mountain Lakes and Streams of the Sierra Nevada", is available through the USDA Forest Service Pacific Southwest Regional Office http://sv0505.rf.fs.fed.us and is widely available at National Forest Interpretive Centers and California Department of Fish and Game offices.

—U.S. Forest Service, Sierra Region web site: http://r05s001.r5.fs.fed.us./ecoregions/m261e. Go to this site and click section "o" on the map. This will bring up an excellent summary of High Sierra geology and ecology. The information is easy to follow, and the site is user-friendly.

## ABOUT THE INHABITANTS

—*California Mountain Wildflowers*, Philip Munz, University of California Press (1963). Meant to be a field key to flower identification. Color photos and line drawings.

—*Discovering Sierra Trees*, Stephen Arno, Yosemite Association (1973). Vignettes about each of the trees the backpacker will encounter. Attractive woodcuts by Jane Geyer convey memorable impressions of the trees.

—*Familiar Trees of North America: Western Region,* Audubon Society, Alfred A. Knopf (1988). Covers all Sierra species; photo illustrated. Small enough to fit comfortably in a shirt pocket. Another one to carry along.

—*Freshwater Fishes of California,* Samuel McGinnis, University of California Press (1984). Intended to be a field key to fish identification, also shows you how it's done. Even includes angling notes and a section on cleaning game fish.

—*Golden Trout of the High Sierra*, Leonard Fisk, State of California Department of Fish and Game (1967). Natural history of the golden trout, including growth cycle and history of D.F.G. involvement in propagation and distribution. Includes angling notes and list of golden trout lakes. (Currently out of print; last printed in 1988, and copies may still be found at D.F.G. offices; Californians, ask your assemblyman to have this updated and republished.)

—*National Audubon Society Nature Guides: Western Forests*, Stephen Whitney, Alfred A. Knopf (Chanticleer 1998). Coverage is Rockies to Pacific, but includes both plant and animal communities, with quick reference indexes and extensive color illustration.

—*Native Trees of the Sierra Nevada*, P. Victor Peterson and P. Victor Peterson, Jr., University of California Press (1975). Meant to be a field key to tree identification. Comprehensive with color plates. Handy pocket size. I carry this one with me.

—*Sierra Nevada Natural History*, Tracy Storer and Robert Usinger, University of California Press (1963). This is one of the best books of its kind ever published. A comprehensive naturalist's handbook every Sierra mountaineer should read, covering geology, climate, flora and fauna (including trout). Plenty of illustrations, including color plates.

—*Trout of California*, J. H. Wales, State of California Department of Fish and Game (1957). Distinguishing characteristics of trout explained, plus notes about their natural history and distribution in California. Color plates of trout. Out of print but a copy of this booklet is online at the D.F.G. web site where you can also view or download the fishing regulations: http://www.dfg.ca.gov/fishing/.

University of California on-line science library: Go to http://elib.cs.berkeley.edu/ and click on Collection Overview, to access photos and descriptions of High Sierra flowers, trees, birds, mammals, amphibians, and insects you are likely to encounter fishing in the High Sierra.

—*Wildflowers 3: The Sierra Nevada*, Elizabeth Horn, Touchstone Press (1976). Field guide organized around habitat. The photo-plus-text-on-same-page format makes this guide easy to use. Even includes brief section on conifers.

## FISH SCIENCE

—*A Trout and Salmon Fisherman for 75 Years*, Edward R. Hewitt, Van Cortlandt Press (1966). First published in the 1940s this is a classic work by a master fisherman and pioneer in the study of trout vision and behavior. Out of print but many editions and reprints available in libraries and used.

—*Complete Brown Trout, The,* Cecil Heacox, Winchester Press (1974). Anatomy and behavior of the brown trout specifically, but much applies to other trout. Includes vignettes about Seth Green and origins of hatcheries, as well as Catskill School of Fly Tying.

—*Fly-fisher's Entomology, The,* Alfred Ronalds, Wellfleet Press (1990). First published in the 1840s the entomology is suspect but not Chapter 1 about trout senses and their "haunts" in the stream. The section on trout vision is illustrated with drawings that diagram the effects of refraction on field of view, and how to apply the fish science to stalk trout.

—*Native Trout of North America,* Robert Smith, Frank Amato Publications (1994). Smith describes his quest to fish for and catch every species and sub-species of trout in North America. Excellent illustrations of the trout and their color variants.

—*Native Trout of Western North America,* Robert Behnke, American Fisheries Society Monograph 6 (1992). Comprehensive taxonomy and discussion of speciation and hybridization issues, with some natural history of western trout. An important scientific work with original conclusions.

—*Through the Fish's Eye,* Mark Sosin and John Clark, Harper & Row (1973). This very readable book relates the behavior and senses of fishes to effective angling technique, lure color, and similar topics. Takes the angler below the surface to the fish's eye level. Would be well worth a second edition to update the science.

—*Trout,* Judith Stoltz and Judith Schnell, Stackpole Books (1991). A compendium of material organized by sections covering evolution, life history and habitat. This is technical material but presented in very understandable language and well illustrated.

—*Trout Biology: An Angler's Guide,* W. B. Willers, University of Wisconsin Press (1981). Anatomy and senses of the trout, genetics and reproduction, and behavior in stream and lake habitats. A classic text and still excellent.

—*Trout Reflections,* David M. Carroll, St. Martin's Press (1993). An almost poetic natural history of the brook trout in small stream habitat. Superb line drawings by the author.

## How to Fly-fish

—*A Primer of Fly-Fishing,* Roderick Haig-Brown, William Morrow & Co. (1964). Well written, comprehensive, with clear line drawings illustrating proper grip and various casts, as well as discussion of methods of presenting flies to trout. (Out of print but found in many libraries.)

—*Trout Fishing,* Joe Brooks, Outdoor Life/Harper & Row (1972). Well-written-and-illustrated how-to book on fly-fishing. Has excellent chapter on grip and basic fly-casting. Also commentary on trout, lake and stream tactics, and flies. Color plates. (Out of print but available used and in libraries.)

## Books about Fly-fishing the High Sierra

—*Desolation Wilderness Fishing Guide,* Jerome Yesavage, Frank Amato Publications (1994). This is an excellent book. The author's comments about fishing Sierra lakes ring true, the descriptions of the waters are easy to follow, and the history of the wilderness is fun to read.

—*Fly Fishing Mammoth,* Mark Heskett, Frank Amato Publications (1994). Terse but the hatch chart tailored to the Eastern Sierra is worth the price of the book.

—*Sierra Trout Guide,* Ralph Cutter, Frank Amato Publications (1991). I gave away my battered and dog-eared copy of the first edition, treasured for its planting charts of lakes and streams, and bought two copies of this book. It is lavishly illustrated with biologically correct color portraits of Sierra trout species, and includes sections on backpacking, flies, hatches and commentary about the fishing. And it includes updated planting charts of Sierra Nevada lakes and streams, which allow you to determine what species are likely to be found in your target lake or stream.

—*Waters of the Golden Trout Country,* Charles McDermand, G.P. Putnam & Sons (1946). Reads almost like an adventure story. He describes fishing for golden trout in waters that you can fish to this day. Heritage type book by a good-hearted man. (Out of print; found in some libraries.)

—*Yosemite and Kings Canyon Trout,* Charles McDermand, G.P. Putnam & Sons (1947). This was first published in 1941 before *Waters.* In this one McDermand relates his conversion to fly-fishing. His descriptions of Yosemite lakes and environs and fishing mountain streams ring true if you have been there and done that. (Out of print, found in some libraries.)

—*Yosemite Trout Fishing Guide,* Steve Beck, Frank Amato Publications (1995). Well-organized, well-written, and very thorough coverage of Yosemite lakes and streams, with a short history of fishing in Yosemite.

## Insects and Selecting Flies

—*Handbook of Hatches,* Dave Hughes, Stackpole Books (1987). Oriented to the western states. Relates each stage of caddis, mayfly and stonefly life cycle to fly patterns. This is the second book to read if you want to tie flies (see below).

—*Hatch Guide for Lakes,* Jim Schollmeyer, Frank Amato Publications (1995). Includes sections on fishing lakes, major insect hatches, the insects' habits and habitat, flies and how to use them. Not specifically for alpine lakes but well worth reading. Small format fits in shirt pocket.

—*Naturals: A Guide to Food Organisms of the Trout,* Gary Borger, Stackpole Books (1980). This is really a fish science book. Covers insects, their molting phases and how to construct naturalistic flies. If you aspire to tie flies, read this book first.

—*Western Hatches: An Angler's Entomology and Fly Pattern Field Guide,* Rick Hafele and Dave Hughes, Frank Amato Publications (1981). Just what the title says. Covers all major insects of interest to fly-fishers in western U.S., habitat, time of emergence and fly patterns. One of the best resources in print for the angler and fly tier.

## Fly-Tying Books

—*American Fly Tying Manual,* Dave Hughes, Frank Amato Publications (1989). This inexpensive handbook is an excellent resource for a beginning fly tier. It covers tools, materials, technique and contains photos and "recipes" for over 300 flies, including the flies on the "A" list.

—*Art of Tying the Wet Fly, The*, James Leisenring, reprinted with Vernon S. Hidy, *Fishing the Flymph*, Crown (1971). A detailed how-to book with clear illustrations. One of the first works in a revolution in the way flies are designed.

—*Soft-Hackled Fly, The*, Sylvester Nemes, Chatham Press (1975). Part of the revolution. This book brought an English tradition of using sparse dressed, soft-hackled flies to the arena. Nemes' book is also a pretty good how-to-tie-flies book, with several classic English patterns included in the tying lessons. Soft-hackled flies are the fly to "go to" in a difficult situation. Recommended highly.

—*Western Trout Fly Tying Manual*, Jack Dennis, Snake River Books (1974). One of the first step-by-step-with-close-up-photos fly-tying books. A classic and still a good place to start. Available in later editions. I studied this book and taught myself to tie flies, using a Noll fly-tying kit. Applying Jack's lessons I could turn out enough Montana Nymphs, Humpies and Rio Grande Kings to fish the Sierras and Trinity Alps. A similar inexpensive kit is currently sold under the Hank Roberts label.

## GETTING THERE: BACKPACKING & TRAILS

—*Backpacking Basics*, Thomas Winnett, Wilderness Press (1979). How to go light. Info about fitting and loading a pack, choosing a campsite and so on is wisdom from someone who knows whereof he speaks. (Later edition available.)

—*High Sierra: John Muir's Range of Light*, Phil Arnot, Wide World Publishing/Tetra (1996). Phil Arnot is, like Muir, a hardened old man of the mountains with a poetic tilt. This excellent book is personal in tone but covers the routes to some of the best high-lake basins and describes what you find. Especially helpful in covering early and late season conditions and travel.

—*High Sierra: Peaks, Passes and Trails, The*, R.J. Secor, The Mountaineers (1992). Secor is a very experienced rock climber and this book covers the highest of the High Sierra. It's a mountaineer's and rock climber's approach book, but the trail descriptions and cross-country routes are useful to an experienced backpacker. (Don't try off-trail travel until you know what you are doing.)

—*Sierra North*, Thomas Winnett, Jason Winnett, Lyn Haber, Kathy Morey, Wilderness Press (1997). 100 mostly High Sierra trips from Mokelumne Wilderness south to Fish Camp. Includes description of trail heads, trails and mention of the fishing at destination. Be sure to read and heed the introductory chapters about wilderness hiking and camping.

—*Sierra South*, Thomas Winnett and Jason Winnett, Wilderness Press (1986). 100 High Sierra trips south of Silver Divide described. See above. Trips 25-100 cover the heart of the High Sierra.

—*Walking Softly in the Wilderness*, John Hart, Sierra Club Books (1984). Comprehensive coverage of backpacking, from fitting your boots to route finding with a compass. Emphasis on wilderness camping. This is a how-to leave-no-trace handbook. (More recent edition available.)

—*Yosemite National Park*, Jeffery Schaffer, Wilderness Press (1989). Trail guide to Yosemite and surrounding wilderness. Includes location of trail heads, difficulty of trails and mention of the fishing at destination. Introductory chapters on history and geology of Yosemite are alone worth the price of this book.

## FLY-FISHING OTHER MOUNTAIN RANGES

**Note:** The Cascades and Rocky Mountains are composed primarily of igneous and metamorphic rock, and granite is a smaller component of the mountains. The higher latitude also means the weather patterns differ and summers are cooler and wetter than in the High Sierra. In general the more alkaline lakes and streams of the Cascades and Rocky Mountains are a more hospitable environment than the oligotrophic lakes of the High Sierra. The rocks matter. In Oregon, despite several plants, golden trout exported from California were unable to establish themselves in the volcanic terrain. In the more granitic alpine wilderness in Montana and Wyoming, golden are established. The world-record golden trout came from the Wind River Range.

—*Alpine Angler*, John Shewey, Frank Amato Publications (1995). Excellent drawings and illustrations of lake structure and cruising routes of alpine trout and good info on what works. Includes well-written section on navigating with a compass.

—*Fly Fishing the High Country*, John Gierach, Pruett Publishing Co. (1984). One of Gierach's first efforts. Has much useful information about fishing Colorado Rockies that carries over to Sierras.

—*Fly Fishing the Mountain Lakes*, Gary LaFontaine, Greycliff Publishing Co. (1998). A mixed bag. Fishing chapters alternate with short stories. But LaFontaine's techniques and approach to fishing are always interesting.

—*Fly Fishing the Rocky Mountain Back Country*, Rich Osthoff, Stackpole Books (1999). The best to date in this genre. A balanced book that covers when, where and how to find trophy trout in the Central Rocky Mountains, particularly the Wind River Range. Doesn't neglect the science either. Highly recommended.

# EPILOGUE

What happened to the young man with the oversized spinning gear I mentioned in the Introduction?

I "loaned" him about two feet of tippet and a soft-hackle fly. Next I had him tie a loop with a slip knot, knot the leader and fly to the loop, and tighten the loop around a chunk of wood. He could cast the fly onto the lake with this rig. Once he got the hang of waiting for the splash to die down, and reeling slowly with plenty of pauses, I left him to fish around the lake.

A half hour or so later, the fading echo of distant whoops of excitement evoked a smile as I crossed over the ridge, headed back to my base camp.